DUMMY RUN

DUMMY RUN

K. R. Wathen

A true, yet unbelievable account of two brother's journey, raising money and awareness for Diabetes, by riding a motorcycle and sidecar around the coast of mainland Britain. The journey turns into disaster, if you're prepared to believe it, 'haunted by the curse of the ventriloquist's dummy?'
A theory opposed by the author, but you have to make up your own mind!

Published by www.lulu.com

DUMMY RUN

ISBN 978-1-291-87266-8

Book formatted by www.bookformatting.co.uk.

Contents

About the Author

Ex scrap man, actor, property developer, T1 diabetic. Loving the writing!

Always had a love of words, unfortunately not always able to put them together in the correct order.

In 2009 Keith suffered a serious nocturnal hypo, causing a seizure which led to a cardiac arrest, he stopped breathing!

Within eight minutes the emergency services arrived but it took a further twenty minutes to get him breathing again.

After twelve days in a coma, during his long recovery he used writing to help work his brain that had been starved of oxygen for so long.

Soon to be published

If Brains Were Gunpowder
Memoirs of a boy

By K R Wathen

Acknowledgement

First of all I would like to thank my brother Ian, for giving up three weeks of his busy life to spend with me on this project, also Ian's wife Vicky for putting up with his absence for the same three weeks.

I would like to show gratitude to our sponsors.

S P Smith Painting Contractors,
Johnstones Paints,
W D Motors
Seven Hills CCTV.

I give a great big thanks to all who donated to our cause and to all the wonderful people who helped us along the way.

I should mention the charity this has all been in aid of.

Living With a Lion
Diabetes Awareness
livingwithalion.com

Most of all I would like to thank Lucy, for saving my life in the first place and for her support and encouragement in taking on this challenge.

The Outfit

Preface

Fifty or sixty years ago, transport was very different to what we see on our roads today, although during the late 1950's, motorcars were becoming cheaper as they were mass-produced. The motorcycle remained a more affordable option and with the addition of the sidecar, it was a very versatile machine. I have very pleasant memories from my childhood of such vehicles in use on the roads. Men travelling to work, taking the family on holiday and outfits with boxes on the chassis for commercial use by people like window cleaners and joiners, even the AA used them for their breakdown service. I have witnessed showmen using the sidecar to transport costumes and props to different venues as they worked the pubs and clubs across the country. So, although I was disturbed when I discovered the contents of my sidecar, I wasn't shocked.

Now, I don't know about you but, I have a strict belief that all inanimate objects, despite their history, are unable to have thoughts or feelings of any kind whatsoever. I know many people think differently about this subject, most of my family are among them, but I cannot allow myself to accept anything as paranormal, when it can be explained by science. However, I wasn't always so set in my mind, as my mum was a firm believer in anything and everything. Throughout my childhood I had ghosts, ghouls, fairies and angels, all looking out for, or over me, watching my every move. With that kind of influence from such a young age, you cannot help but believe in all sorts of weird and wonderful things. Then I grew up! As I grew older and wiser, I was forced by my own intelligence to question these claims.

When I set out to write this book, I did not intend to question the meaning of life, but seeing as we're here, I will give you my account.

Although I do not fully understand the physics and the chemistry behind the creation of the universe, I do believe in it, and I'm afraid that God does not enter into any of it. Having said that, if you are a religious person, then please, don't chuck the book! I have a great admiration for the intention of religion. However, to put it in simple terms, I believe that most religions were brought about to, guide and help us through the difficult journey of life as a source of comfort and inspiration. A typical example would be the Ten Commandments, ten Ideal rules that, if everyone on earth adhered to, would ensure a perfect life for us all. Unfortunately we humans do not always adhere well. Which leaves religion open to the misinterpretation of many, self obsessed people who, throughout the ages, seem to have murdered and maimed, not just individuals but entire nations, and continue to persecute, even now in the twenty first century, all in the name of religion.

As for reincarnation, another strong belief of many, my theory is as follows.

There is life after death, but it is the life we create here on Earth before we die. We live on through our children. How simple is that? The meaning of life explained by a bloke from Yorkshire!

I do not intend to challenge any of the wonderful religions across the world; I am simply giving you an insight as to the workings of my mind. However, after the events of the summer of 2013, I was forced to reconsider my beliefs.

When giving a short account of our experiences during that summer, to friends and family, I am always met with the same response.

"You couldn't write this sort of stuff, you should write a book!"

A statement, that continues to confuse me. Nevertheless I took the advice.

Chapter one

A feeling of being enclosed, as I woke to the sound of voices from my childhood, wrapped like a package, tightly packed in an envelope, surrounded by bubble wrap, as if I were about to be sent on a journey. Unable to move my arms, I struggled to break free. With sweat forming on my brow, I wriggled about like a madman in a straight jacket, locked in his padded cell.

"Keith! What are you doing?"

The sound of Lucy's voice calmed me, enabling me to realise that the straight jacket was in fact a 'mummy' style sleeping bag and the padded cell, a very small two person tent. I had turned over and over in the same direction, causing the sleeping bag to tighten around me like a twisted dishcloth.

"I know how a mummy feels now!"

I replied, as I reverse rolled a couple of times, releasing the grip of the sleeping bag and allowing my arms to break free.

It was the morning of Saturday August 3rd 2013 and I was indeed about to embark on a journey. The two man tent was to be my home for the following three weeks but, rather than enjoying the tiny space with my dear wife, I would be sharing it with my younger, although much larger brother, Ian.

Two male siblings form a brood of seven, aged seven years apart. Ian in his late forties and me, Keith in my middle fifties, had decided to take on a mammoth motorcycling challenge, to ride around the coast of mainland Britain on an old motorcycle and sidecar combination.

"You must be mad!"

"Stark raving bonkers!"

Was the type of response we received, don't get me wrong, most admired the reason behind our madness, they simply believed we should, perhaps use something a little newer, for such an enormous task. After all, it was around four thousand miles, following the coast road from the Humber Bridge in a clockwise direction, until we arrive back at the Bridge three weeks later. But it was to be a fund raising event, raising money and awareness for diabetes.

After living with diabetes myself for twenty seven years, in December 2009 I had a serious nocturnal hypoglycaemia, which caused me to have a seizure. I fell out of bed and began to spill blood from a head wound as I hit the bedside cabinet. I then stopped breathing and had a cardiac arrest, at this point I became motionless and to all intents and purposes, I had died! My life was saved by the fast actions of my wife, who immediately called the emergency services and followed the instructions she was given. Paramedics arrived on the scene after eight minutes but it took a further twenty minutes to get me breathing again. I was taken to hospital where I remained in a coma for the following twelve days.

Recovery was a slow process, made worse by deep vein thrombosis and a pulmonary embolism (blood clots, leg and lung), I also sustained six fractured vertebrae after a couple of falls and was later diagnosed with osteoporosis. So all in all, I had been having a bit of a shit time of it!

The following twelve months were pretty grim, I felt useless, like a crippled, crumbling wreck unable to do every day chores. I fell into a deep depression. I now feel for my wife and family, for how they must have felt at the time, wondering whether I would live or die.

I needed something to keep me busy, something to make my brain work harder, after it had been starved of oxygen for so long and something to help rebuild muscle that had deteriorated so quickly. I started to dabble with creative writing which helped with the brain, but I needed something more physical. I found the answer in a Royal Enfield motorcycle, a 500 Bullet and I spent the next twelve months replacing parts, cleaning, painting and polishing my new acquisition, until it had the look and feel of a true English motorcycle, even though it had been manufactured in Madras, India in 1995.

Royal Enfield motorcycles were produced in England throughout the whole of the first half of the twentieth century, supplying not only the British forces but also the Imperial Russian government, and in 1949, they received an order from the Indian government, for eight hundred 350cc Bullets. The Redditch based company, formed a partnership with Madras Motors to form 'Enfield India' who assembled the 350 bullets under licence in Madras, all of the parts were manufactured in England and shipped to India to be assembled. In 1957 the tooling was bought by Enfield India, enabling them to manufacture components in India. Enfield India continued to make these motorcycles, both 350 and 500cc models and in 1986 they began exporting them to England. In 1994 Eicher Group bought into Enfield India and in 1995 they acquired rights to the name 'Royal Enfield' and still produce similar model motorcycles today, selling in over twenty different countries.

Well, that's enough about the history! This is a story about the journey and some of the weird encounters we were about to witness.

It all began during a pleasant evening spent at my brother's house, while enjoying a glass of wine after our evening meal. I had gone there to help with some building work and decided to stay over to avoid the one hour drive home. Our discussions covered many subjects, before eventually finding their way around to death. We spoke of how Ian's wife Vicky had lost her brother Andrew to diabetes in the year 2000, aged just thirty five. He had lived with diabetes most of his life before sadly dying from kidney failure, one of the main complications of long term diabetes. Inevitably conversation found it's way to my close encounter which prompted Ian to ask.

"What is the one thing you would like to achieve before you die?"

To which I replied.

"I would like to travel around the coast of mainland Britain on a motorcycle, setting off from any given point on the coast and riding until I arrive back where I started."

I could see that Ian was impressed by my ambition and I'm sure if I'd have looked closely, I would have seen the cogs beginning to turn inside his head as he replied.

"Well, do it! You've got the bike, get yourself off."

The remainder of that evening was spent laughing and joking about the good and bad possibilities that may occur during such a challenge, as well as suggestions of a variety of contraptions one could use as a form of transport to make such a journey. Trying to recall all of the conversation that night is difficult as the wine did flow, I do remember something about a pogo stick, but most of all I remember vividly, the point when Ian suggested we attach a sidecar to the bike and do it together, following that came the icing on the cake when he suggested we do it to raise money for diabetes.

The next morning, in the cold light of day, we reflected on our conversation the night before and could only agree, it was a cracking idea! Our only problem now was to convince the wives.

K. R. WATHEN

Who could resist that smile?

Chapter two

I now had a new focus in life, we had one year to plan and promote our new venture. First of all, we needed a sidecar. Ian often stayed over at my house when working in the area, and during one of his stays, while scanning the sidecar category on eBay, we spotted it. We immediately agreed. This was the one! It was a Watsonian Avonair sports sidecar, circa early sixties, in need of some TLC. After some outbidding, we finally placed the winning bid and YIPEE! We were on our way. We rescued the rotting sidecar from a garden in North Wales and took it home. The following day Ian returned to work and I began the refurbishing operation.

While working on the sidecar, I noticed a small boot compartment, accessible from behind the single seat. I removed the seat and putting my hand through a small hole in the ply, I felt a catch. A quick flick and the boot lid came open. The air filled with a damp musty odour and inside was what looked like a crumpled wax jacket. It turned out to be the canvas hood cover and as I removed it I noticed a small foot, complete with shoe. Cautiously, I unwrapped the canvas and saw 'Charlie' for the first time, his jaw dropped as I attempted to free him and his hideous face came into full view. My immediate reaction was one of fear, through my very distant memory of 'Dead Of Night' A portmanteau television horror film in black and white, where one episode was the story of a possessed ventriloquists dummy. I felt a shiver run down my spine as the hairs on my body stood to attention in a futile attempt to protect me.

After gathering myself together, I took in a deep breath and paced a few steps in a circling motion, saying to myself.

"It's only a doll you idiot, get a grip!"

Charlie was indeed a ventriloquist's dummy, an inanimate object with no ability to cause me any harm, yet his company disturbed me.

I now feel a need to stop referring to a mouldy old doll as a person, with a name, but how else would I be able to tell my story? So, I will continue to refer to him as 'Charlie' even though, it's just a dummy! That still sends shivers down my spine as I write these words.

Meet Charlie

I put Charlie to one side, hung by the scruff of his neck on the garage wall. I had decided to face my demons every day while I worked on the sidecar and I have to admit, despite being watched over by a scary puppet, the end result was spectacular. When I hitched the sidecar to the bike it looked like it was meant to be there. I was so proud of my outfit and enjoyed learning to ride it. As anyone who has driven a hack will know, it is very different from riding a solo motorcycle, but I took to it like a duck to water. I now had to focus on creating and promoting a suitable charity.

We had decided that with such a lot of work and effort going into this, we wanted to know exactly where the money we raised would be going, the only way to ensure this was to organise and run our own charity. One that would be all about diabetes. First of all we needed a name. My first instincts were to use a short story I had written. Remember the creative writing bit? The story is a metaphor, comparing life with diabetes and my experiences, to living with a lion. And here it is...

Living With a Lion

Imagine being told that you have to spend the rest of your life in the company of a lion. You are not particularly zoologically minded and have no desire to do such a ridiculous thing, but you are given no choice in the matter, you are simply presented with instructions on how to live with this potential killer. It is explained to you that you have to look after this creature and always have its welfare in mind; the two of you then could have a long and happy life together. However, you must always be aware that if you neglect or mistreat this new partner, the consequences could be fatal!

Your instructions include the fact that the lion will be with you twenty four hours a day, seven days a week and fifty two weeks of the year. You must be aware that he is a hungry lion and will need regular feeding, if you fail to maintain his feeding and he becomes very hungry, he may decide to eat you. At the same time, he must not be over fed as this will result in him becoming very grumpy and tired. In this condition he will become a heavy burden for you to drag around, so heavy in fact, after several years of tugging around this over fed lion, you will start to suffer health problems that could shorten your life.

So, given all of this information, you set out to build a relationship with the mighty lion and all goes well, apart from when you forget to feed him and he attempts to eat you, or you give him too much food and have to live with his grumpiness. This up and down relationship goes on through the years of your life and all in all, you and the lion appear to get along fine.

After many years and several close shaves, one night you go to bed at a time when the lion has not had enough to eat and he has no choice but to have another attempt at eating you. This time you have underestimated his hunger and therefore you suffer the unimaginable consequences. Somehow you manage to survive the attack and are rushed to hospital in an unconscious, half eaten state, where you are miraculously put back together and there you remain for a long time during your recovery.

When you eventually regain enough strength to leave the hospital, you are given a lead and when you enquire what it is, you are told. "It's your lion, and hey, try and be a bit more careful with him this time."…….. Aaaaaaaaaargh!!!!!

By the way, I have a lion; his name is 'Diabetes Mellitus'
A short story by K R Wathen
I used the name of my story to set up the charity 'Living With a Lion' which we now had to promote, along with the 'Classic Coastal Sidecar Challenge' which was the name we gave our ambitious journey.

With the outfit suitably sign written, we began attending classic car and bike shows, village fetes and any public gathering that would have us. Cash started to come in and we had to open a bank account. Something, much more difficult than you could possibly imagine. An otherwise simple procedure until you mention the word 'charity' but some things have to be done correctly and this was one of them.

At one particular venue, a local summer fair, where they were holding a classic car and bike show, I made a last minute decision to attend. As I would be going alone on this occasion, I decided to take Charlie with me, simply to judge people's reactions.

The field was a hustle of people, in and out of stalls, playing traditional games and eating everything from ice cream to homemade pork pies. I was parked among a range of classic vehicles in a line of old motorcycles. While engaged in a conversation with a lady about her diabetes, I was interrupted by a man, probably in his sixties with greying hair, quite tall, wearing a short sleeved shirt and trousers. He asked.

"Is it your bike?"

"Yes it is."

I replied, a little taken aback by his lack of consideration for my existing conversation.

"Does he talk?"

He went on, pointing to Charlie. I looked to my side, at the doll and back to this man who seemed to care nothing for anything or anyone else at this time. I reached down to the sidecar and picked up Charlie with my hand inside his back and brought him toward me.

"What's your name?"

Charlie asked in a high pitched voice, his mouth opening and closing in sync with the words that came from my stomach.

"Harry."

The man answered, before turning to me and announcing.

"It sounds just like my mother."

Charlie moved forward toward the man, his eyes moved downward looking at the man's feet before slowly raising up, inspecting the whole of his body. He stopped, staring in to the man's eyes, as he spoke.

"I am your mother Harold!"

Charlie spoke in a soft tone which quickly became harsh as he went on.

"And what do you think you're playing at? Swanning about this place like Lord Muck when you should be at home looking after your sister. I can't turn me back for two minutes before you're up to something. You'll be the death o' me our Harold!"

Blood drained from the man's face, his jaw dropped and tears welled in his eyes. After a moment of shocked silence, the man became agitated, almost panicking as he spoke directly to Charlie.

"You're already dead!... You can't hurt me!.."

He turned his attention to me.

"Why are you doing this? She's dead!... This is sick, you're sick!... He's sick!"

With his quivering hand pointing at Charlie he turned on his heels and took his shaking body into the crowd.

I pulled the doll off my hand and threw it into the sidecar. The lady I had been speaking with, having witnessed the whole thing, asked.

"Do you know him?"

Still dazed, I told her.

"I've never seen him before in my life!"

With a look of terror on her face the lady cupped her cheeks in her hands, exclaiming.

"Oh my god!"

She too then disappeared into the crowd. I quickly gathered my things together, threw them into the sidecar, kicked up the bike and headed home.

I have no idea why the stranger reacted the way he did, nor have I any idea why I said what I said to him, but it felt weird, I was even tempted to throw the dummy out of the sidecar on the way home, but knowing my luck, I'd be nicked for littering the highway.

I know this story can sound strange, and it may just be coincidence, I may have said just enough to upset the man, it may be that the man had a mother who sounded like my very amateur ventriloquists voice. I don't know and probably never will, but I do know that on returning home I looked up ventriloquism on the internet and learned that the word comes from the Latin words, venter, meaning belly and loqui meaning speak. 'To speak from the belly.' In ancient times the act was considered to be a way of communicating with the dead. There is evidence of Necromancy as far back as the sixth century and in many places it was illegal, punishable by death! By the sixteenth century it was used as a form of amusement and by the eighteenth century it was used across Europe as popular entertainment. However, there have always been doubters. And even today it continues to scare the pants off a lot of people.

As the summer came to an end and the nights became longer, the outfit spent more and more time parked in the garage under the watchful eye of Charlie. I used the winter months to upgrade a lot of parts on the bike like, stronger springs in the front forks, a heavy duty clutch, new tyres, new brake drums and shoes, new cables and wheel bearings. I had to lower the gear ratio, to compensate for the weight of the sidecar. So, with new chain and sprockets fitted, a selection of spare parts acquired to accompany us, we fixed a date for our trip. Saturday 3rd August 2013.

Because most of the decisions we made usually took place in my garage, they were often witnessed by Charlie, who sometimes seemed to hold a very disapproving look. Not all of the time, it must have been the different angles I saw him from. Creating an assortment of expressions, but wherever I was when I cast him a glance he was always staring intensely at me! It's amazing how you can allow your mind to consider illogical reasoning sometimes, but without doubt, it definitely felt like Charlie was not with us on this one. It had become a joke between Ian and myself when together in the garage, comments would often be made, like.

"Careful, Charlie's listening."

Or.

"Oh dear, Charlie doesn't look happy with that idea."

All of which was said in a very light hearted way yet, for a dummy that has no capacity for feelings, Charlie seemed to be making his very clear!

Chapter three

Squeezing myself out of my straight jacket, I searched for the zip to the padded cell. The voices I could hear were those of my family and friends, some of them my sisters, some nephews and nieces; they were accompanied by the clanking of bottles and the crushing of empty beer cans. I found the zip, enabling me to let in some sunlight and much needed fresh air. Sticking my head out of the tent, I was greeted by an array of various sized, shaped and coloured tents covering the ground like a serious skin condition covers the body. In between the lumps and bumps were people I Knew, busying themselves in an attempt to remove all evidence of enjoyment from the night before. Through my, not quite focused eyes, they appeared like bacteria buzzing around the inflammations that were their tents.

Everyone had gathered together to give us a bit of a send off the evening before at the Humber Bridge Water Ski Club, where Ian and Vicky were members. Friends and family had joined us and set up their tents in a corner of the field that was already occupied by an army of very angry ants, who tended to bite any intruders of their territory.

The Enfield was positioned in front of the club house, overlooking the lake which made a beautiful setting. We had enjoyed a hog roast, given by way of a donation and a good time was had by all. But now it was time to face reality, we were here for a purpose and the clock was ticking.

The only way out of the tent was to crawl on my hands and knees, like a prisoner of war making his escape, which is what I did after I had awkwardly pulled on some clothes. The feeling of open space was welcomed as I stretched my stiff limbs. By now the camping stoves were assembled and water nearing the boil for that essential first cup of tea. I searched for my brother and eventually found him, as cosy as a piece of toast in the back of a camper van!

Our next location was the official designated point from where we would commence our journey, The Humber Bridge viewing area, chosen for its picturesque views over the Humber Estuary with the magnificent concrete and steel structure that is the Humber Bridge, stretching over the water and holding itself, so that we humans may cross the vast expanse.

I was beginning to feel nervous as we packed our belongings into the panniers and the small space that had been Charlie's home for so long. We fitted a camera to the front of the bike and with suitable clothing and helmets on, Ian gave the kick start a couple of tries before it burst into life and with its heavy beat as the single cylinder engine pounded its piston up and down, letting out a throb of sound from the exhaust. It is always a relief when the engine fires up, especially when you have such a large audience of critical relatives. Ian jumped on the bike, I climbed in the sidecar and we were on our way.

Cameras began clicking as we entered the viewing area, where we took up several positions to pose for the photographers, holding up banners to promote our charity and our sponsors, but during all of this time I was longing to be as far away from anyone as we knew as we could possibly be, purely so I would be saved from any embarrassment in the event of a breakdown.

Eventually, after being admired, well wished, advised and waved goodbye, we were now, really on our way.

Chris, a friend and fellow type one diabetic had fitted the camera to the bike and decided to follow us for the first few mile, sometimes overtaking us and stopping ahead to capture a few images as we passed. The first part of our journey led us close to where Ian lives and we stopped to pick up those inevitable few bits that he had forgotten to pack, after which we were 'really' on our way.

Passing through familiar villages we eventually reached an open road, where Ian twisted the throttle. The feeling was exhilarating as our speed increased, sat in a tiny container attached to the side of a 500cc motorcycle, open to the elements with wind rushing past us. It couldn't get much better when the rear wheel of the bike suddenly stopped turning, causing a screeching sound as the tyre scraped across the tarmac. We free wheeled as Ian instinctively pulled in the clutch lever and shouted to me.

"It's fuckin' seized up!"

"Oh Bollocks!"

I replied politely as we slowly ground to a halt.

Six miles into our incredible journey and the engine had seized. Twelve months of planning and promoting. One year of preparation and intense effort and after a measly six miles we were stuck at the side of the road. I glanced to my left where, silhouettes of an Immingham oil refinery lie between us and the Humber Estuary. My head fell into my hands and for a second or two I wished the ground would open up and swallow me whole. I then had a reality check and almost in unison, two brothers leapt from the bike.

Taking off our jackets and helmets we set about doing what we do best. In no time at all the petrol tank and exhaust were on the floor, Ian began shouting abuse as he rummaged under the seat of the sidecar, something about the lack of a socket set. In times of crisis, we stick together, we work together to put things right and we shout at each other to let off steam. I had carefully selected a few chosen tools that would allow us to do almost any work we should encounter and would fit into the small space under the seat of the sidecar. However Ian decided he needed a mechanics full tool kit to work with.

After a 'calm down' moment, Ian decided to go with Chris who was still following at this point, to buy some tools while I remained with the bike and removed the cylinder head without any need of a socket set. The engine was now turning freely, I assumed because it had cooled sufficiently and no damage seemed to have been done. Using a new head gasket that I had remembered to bring with us, I began the reassembling operation. I was joined by a passing cyclist who offered his assistance along with the use of the garage at the side of his nearby house and a nice cup of tea. I declined his offer and he left me with a great admiration of his generosity.

Before Ian and Chris returned, two cars pulled up, I looked in wonder of who it could be. I then recognised the two blokes walking toward me followed by their wives. It was my nephew Chris and his mate Lloyd. I took a deep breath, filling my lungs with defensive confidence as they asked.

"Is everything ok?"

"Of course it is, we're just having a few teething troubles, nothing to worry about."

I answered. They looked at the bike and the pile of bits scattering the grass verge and with an element of doubt in their voices replied.

"OK, er… We'll just er… leave you to it.. then… Are you sure?

"Of course I am, go on get yourselves off."

I convinced them.

Ian and Chris returned with a selection of shiny new tools and Ian complained of the £80 he had spent on them, something he continues to remind me of even to this day. Before long, after a couple of hiccups with the de-compression valve becoming bent, we were finally back on the road. The engine sounded as good as ever and I began to relax in the sidecar, but not for long. After about the same distance, the same thing happened. The tyre screeched, we free wheeled to a stop. This time we attempted to alter the ignition timing, in hope that the engine would run a little cooler, after all it was the middle of a hot summer and the bike was carrying far more weight than it was intended for.

We set off again, and it seized again, we fiddled with the timing, set off again and it seized again. Eventually we discovered that if we restricted our speed to 38mph or less we could achieve greater distances. Before long, Chris left us, believing we would now be ok, he headed home, somewhere we wouldn't be seeing for a while.

Because of the delays, we knew we had no chance of reaching Lowestoft, which was our first chosen overnight stop and where a welcome party had been arranged for us, as it was getting late, we decided to make an unscheduled stop, close to Boston. We followed signs for a campsite, taking us off the main road and toward a very nice place known as the Pilgrims Way Camping Site. Our entrance was blocked by a barrier, we parked the bike and walked the short distance to reception, we were met by the owner who welcomed us to stay but refused to let us pay, as a way of supporting our charity. We were let in with the bike and shown our allocated spot where we pitched our tent. After a quick wash and brush up, we headed to the local pub for a decent meal.

The food was good and the company, interesting! We ended up talking to a fellow biker, who listened to our tales of woe and told us of the love hate relationship he had with his Harley Davidson. One that sounded just like the one we had passed as we entered the pub car park. When I say this it means nothing until I explain the condition of this man, he was so drunk he could barely stand, his speech was so slurred it was barely recognisable as English apart from the odd word that filtered through. At the end of the evening, as the biker collected his helmet from behind the bar, Ian looked at me shaking his head and said.

"He can't be riding it.. Can he?"

I didn't answer immediately I simply watched as the drunken biker left the pub, I then suggested.

"He's probably gonna walk home and pick up the bike in the morning."

With that, the unmistakable sound of the V twin told us different, we ran outside and witnessed the bike and rider gliding perfectly out of the car park onto the main road and disappearing into the distance as the roar of the V twin faded.

Following that, I rode the outfit back to the campsite sober, where we were met by a problem we had already experienced earlier. The barrier was down and we had no card to open it. After a couple of failed attempts at wangling the bike around the post we gave up. Walking into the site we were met by a pleasant man who offered us the use of his card to raise the barrier and we pushed the bike into the site, so as not to disturb other campers.

Our allocated plot was close to the entrance; we parked the bike and partly undressed before entering into our temporary accommodation. It was a struggle to say the least, for the two of us to squeeze into such a tiny space. Eventually we settled down, but something wasn't right. Ian didn't settle quite as much as he should and began tossing and turning like a beached whale. It soon became clear that he was in a panic as he fought to unzip the tent.

"I can't stand it! I need air! I need to get out!"

He said struggling with the zip. As soon as he undid the tent he calmed instantly, taking in a deep breath of night air. I was slightly shocked by Ian's display, but I did understand the way he felt.

"I didn't know you suffered with claustrophobia."

I said, to which he replied.

"Neither did I!"

You learn something new every day, I thought as I stuffed ear plugs into my ears and turned over. Ian closed up the tent and assured me that the panic was over and he was now fine.

When sharing a space smaller than a single bed with another person, who you know snores, equally as loud as yourself; it is a good thing to have a supply of ear plugs.

After a good night's sleep we were up early enjoying breakfast of tea and toast, cooked on a single burner camping stove, when Ian told me of events during the night, after I had gone to sleep. He explained that a group of people with tents pitched next to ours were enjoying a drink outside, late in the evening, when I began snoring. They began to get annoyed with the noise and remarked loudly about the volume of my slumbering sound, they even made comparisons to the sound of the motorcycle engine. As their drinking continued they began bickering between themselves about the one of them that had allowed us to use his card to get in. Eventually, as my snoring had been the source of their entertainment for long enough, they retired to their beds, and here is the best bit. According to Ian, one of them started to snore, even louder than me!

With tent packed away, bike and sidecar loaded up, we took to the road. This time I was on the bike with Ian beside me in the chair, I tickled the throttle, managing to travel a fair distance before the inevitable happened. Yes, you guessed it, the damn thing seized again. I managed to coast along the flat road until we reached a turn off where I pulled off the main road and stopped on a grass verge. Ian climbed out of the sidecar, took the luggage off the boot rack and began rummaging in the boot.

"We're not stripping it again.

I said with despair.

"No, I'm putting the kettle on."

He replied with a beaming smile on his face as he took out the camping stove and began setting it up on the grass.

"Go and see if you can get some milk." He ordered, pointing toward a nearby house. We had binned the bottle we bought that morning in case of spillage. I obeyed the order without question, although I did wonder as I walked down the very typically English country lane, how insane it would seem to anyone answering the door to a middle aged man wearing motorcycle clothing, asking for milk. I knocked at the door and waited; eventually a young woman opened the door with a puzzled look on her face and said.

"Yes?"

"Do you have any milk you could spare us?

I asked in a timid voice.

"No! We don't have milk, we don't use it."

She insisted before closing the door rather sharper than it was opened. Of all the houses in the whole of Britain, I chose to beg for milk at the one that doesn't use milk. I tried again at the neighbouring property, no one was in. I was beginning to feel as if everything was against us and I gave up, returning to Ian, who had boiled the water and was waiting for the milk. I explained how I had failed to get milk, Ian got up off his knees and with a look of disappointment said.

"Get out of the way, If you want anything doing, do it yourself!"

Pushing past me, he positively stomped his way down the lane muttering to himself and before long, returned with the much needed milk and we enjoyed a lovely cup of tea over enough time for the engine to cool sufficiently.

When planning this trip we set out a list of places where we would stay overnight on each day our travels, as well as making brief stops at some of the seaside towns in order to rattle our collection buckets. So far we had done none of this as we were already a day behind and it was only our second day!

I decided to make a stop at Cromer, it was lunch time and I felt a little peckish. I found a space on the sea front to park the bike, after dismounting I attempted to straighten the thing up but we were on a hill and the bike rolled forward crashing into a wall, damaging the paint on the sidecar. I didn't care anymore. A leisurely stroll around the town and a delicious roast chicken sandwich was all it needed to cheer us up. Back at the bike, with helmets and jackets on I kicked down on the start lever, it refused to start, several attempts later, in the heat of the day I was beginning to melt. Ian tapped me on the leg and pointed down the hill shouting.

"Try bump starting it!"

Good idea, I thought and allowed the outfit to roll forward, the hill was fairly steep but not so long and I barely reached enough speed before we ran out of hill. Luckily, as I let out the clutch the engine came to life and I spun the bike around, making a hasty exit, away from the embarrassment of the on looking crowd.

As we travelled south the engine was not sounding too good, it had developed a rattle, which eventually became a knock and the knock grew louder, it was without doubt the big eng bearing and it became so bad that eventually we had to stop. We were close to a place called Southwold, about twenty five miles north of Ipswich and I pulled the machine into a petrol station / mini supermarket. It had a large car park where I parked the bike and we took off the cylinder head and barrel. Our suspicions were correct, the big end had disintegrated and we were knackered!

Ian had been working for most of the year in Clacton and was still based down there, he had his caravan on a site and his wife was staying there running the business, fitting central heating systems on a large estate. He telephoned Vicky and asked her to send one of the workers with a pickup to come and collect us. Our next stop after Lowestoft was going to be Clacton, so we decided to go there and find a replacement engine.

We had a long wait for the pickup to arrive and during that time many people came and went for shopping or fuel, occasionally people would admire the bike, or what we were doing or both. Some people put coins in our collection tin and one bloke reached in his carrier bag and took out two bottles of beer, saying.

"You look like you need a drink lads."

We did! And gratefully accepted. Another man came over to us, introducing himself in broken English.

"Hello, my name is Sven, I am Shwedish, from Shweden, I am also riding the motorshycles, English bikes BSA in the fairgrounds, 'Wall of Death.' Not any more, but I did before. We had the sidecar too, and a lion, yes it is true, with the lion in the sidecar on the 'Wall of Death.' What is wrong with your motorshycle?

"We need a new engine, the big end has gone!"

I explained.

"No problems, I know a man with all of the parts you will need! He is my friend, he has a garage full of English motorshycle, he never will sell anything, but he will give them to you, I will telephone him."

Sven handed me his phone, it was still ringing out, someone answered and I attempted to explain our needs to a complete stranger, over the phone. The man on the phone was confused; he wanted to know how Sven's name had come up as the caller. I filled him in with the details and he told me.

"I do have some motorbike parts, but not what you need and why the hell is that nut case telling you I have!?"

Sven left us, apologising for being unable to help, we thanked him and will definitely never forget him.

The petrol station closed and the shop soon after, we were left, waiting. Ian found a bench where he laid himself out and I sat on the ground among a pile of engine parts wondering, if that scruffy little dummy was still hung on the garage wall with a smirk on its face!

The pickup arrived, followed by Vicky in her car. After loading the bike and the pile of spares we set sail for Clacton on Sea. It was getting late as we approached Clacton and we called at a KFC for some grub. During the short journey we had left, following the pickup in the car I noticed the bike had broken loose from its limited fastenings, two luggage straps to be precise, all we had available. I heard the rear light lens on the bike break as it hit the head board of the truck, as we pulled up at traffic lights I quickly jumped out of the car and onto the back of the pickup, grabbing hold of the front wheel of the bike and laying down along side it with my foot under the rear wheel, preventing it from moving backward or forward. I held this position for the last couple of mile of the journey. I had a panic moment when I heard sirens and saw flashing blue lights as the truck slowed down, but fortunately only to allow the police car past. We finally arrived at the caravan site where we unloaded the bike and took advantage of a proper bed by enjoying a good night's sleep, well almost a proper bed!

Chapter four

Having searched the internet for what seemed like an eternity, we located a number of second hand engines. One was close to Bristol but lacking a cylinder head. Another was in Birmingham and slightly over priced, even with charity discount it was still £1000 and the one we opted for was in Cheadle, asking price £500 with our old engine in exchange.

The engine was stripped from the bike in no time and placed in the boot of Vicky's car ready for the journey to Cheadle, which is close to Stoke on Trent and a long way from Clacton.

After making the decision to do this challenge, we had discussed the possibility of major breakdown and agreed that no matter how bad it was, we could fix it. Our dad was a mechanic, and in 1945 he set up his own business, repairing and dismantling cars, the dismantling eventually took priority and he focused himself in that direction. Selling spare parts and weighing the remainder in for scrap, in other words he ran a scrap yard or auto salvage company, if you like. Ian and I, along with our older brother all worked at the yard from leaving school until it finally closed in 1997. Our experience in the yard meant we both had considerable knowledge of the internal combustion engine and much more, so we weren't about to give up yet. However, we had misdiagnosed the first engine fault, believing it to be an overheating problem when it turned out to be a worn oil pump drive, seizing the engine on the rocker shafts, before eventually knocking out the big end bearing.

John was the gentleman we were looking for in Cheadle. During our telephone conversation I mentioned the fact that we were on a charity run, to which he replied.

"I don't do charity!"

We found his place and could see that he earned his living out of Royal Enfield motorcycles from his back garden and shed and we understand that everyone has to make a living.

After meeting John, we realised that he was a helpful sort of bloke and he did want to strip the engine before letting us take it. But we were in a rush and John didn't seem like he did anything in too much of a hurry. So we agreed to take the engine as it was. John had previously owned the bike that the engine came from and was assured when buying it back, it was as good as when he had owned it before. We agreed on a price of £450 and John threw in a gasket set, sparkplug, oil filter, oil pump drive and even a new rear lamp.

Back to Clacton in the pouring rain and dinner in the clubhouse, where the night before, another welcoming party had been arranged and we had sadly missed, again!

The following day, putting the bike back together took a little longer than expected, so we stayed a third night in Clacton. The bike was running but as it was so late we decided to make a fresh start the following day. To celebrate, we went out for a meal. Ian and Vicky, Ian's daughter Julia and myself, a pub was mentioned and we drove the few miles to the Robin Hood, where after Ian ripped the arse out of his shorts getting out of the car, we settled down and ordered our meals. Chicken Forrestierre in my case and I was looking forward to it. I searched for my insulin pen and realised I had forgotten to bring it. Hardly ever being able to eat anything without injecting insulin, you would think that I would always be aware of the need to have it with me and I usually am. But sometimes, especially if I am out of my normal routine, I can forget the most important item for me, when going out for a meal, which is of course insulin. I had to beg the use of the car and return to the campsite, pick up the necessary and return to the Robin Hood, where my meal awaited me and was thoroughly enjoyed. Our waitress for the evening turned out to be something of an entertainer, performing 'The Otter Dance' for our table. Picture if you will Kim, a young female waitress performing a song and dance routine, she had learned in infant school, in the middle of a busy pub. I mention this because it was just the sort of light hearted ingredient we needed to lift our spirits.

The next day we were up early with our bags packed and ready to go. With the new engine sounding good, we were ready to rock and roll. We set off, oozing with confidence and looking forward to the thousands of miles ahead of us.

We didn't get far! Approximately six or eight miles before there were signs of the cylinder head gasket going. We pulled up at the side of the road, removed the tank and exhaust, then the cylinder head. We replaced the gasket with the one John had supplied us with and reassembled the machine. A few miles down the road we stopped and retightened the head bolts, just to be on the safe side.

We managed to reach the south east corner of England where we stopped off to take a look over the white cliffs of Dover, we admired the castle as we passed and continued along the south coast. We passed through Hastings and Eastbourne, but the bike had begun to lose power. I had to use the gearbox more when travelling uphill. This was not a good sign, oil was leaking from the engine. It was looking like head gasket trouble again.

Our next scheduled stop was near Brighton, where Julia's boyfriend, Sam lived with his parents. We were struggling to keep going and we stopped on a main road at a place called Romney, outside an Indian restaurant and opposite a car spares shop, which was handy as we had lost the rear light lens somehow. We purchased a trailer light and cobbled it to fit, as well as a tub of hand cleaner, a bag of rags and some gasket sealing compound that we thought may help with our troubles. The bike was stripped yet again to remove the head gasket, but when we came to replacing it we realised the only gasket we now had was for a 350cc and considerably smaller. As the gasket was not torn apart we were able to rescue and re-use it along with a dollop of gasket goo!

While fixing the bike we were joined by a couple of guys from the Indian restaurant who watched as we worked. I attempted to coerce them into supplying us with some food, using guilt as my tools, explaining how it was their fault we were there, because the bike was built in India. It didn't work, we remained hungry.

During our trip so far I had realised and learned a couple of things. One was why they called bikers, 'Greasers' the answer is because they are always covered in greasy black oil! Another one was why people refer to motorcycles as 'She' or 'Her' as if they were female. The answer to that one is obvious, because they can be real bitches!

With the bike reassembled we set off again with our hearts in our mouths. We had one more stop to make, for food and we found a fish and chip shop on a hill, which would allow us to bump start if necessary. The meal was most enjoyable, sitting on the pavement outside the chip shop, where the proprietor had given us a fiver for our charity. Worthing was our next target and we had it in our sights as we approached the outskirts of the town, we were on a sort of twisty, flyover, bypass piece of road and as the light was fading, with the exhaust glowing red hot, the engine suddenly died. We had run out of petrol! Ordinarily this wouldn't have been a problem as we were carrying a spare five litre jerry can with us, but we were losing compression and leaking oil badly and the bike hadn't a cat in hell's chance of starting without a tow. We free wheeled down the twisting road until we found a place where we could pull off. We seemed to be under a sort of spaghetti junction, lit by sodium street lights.

Emptying the jerry can of spare fuel into the bike, the sound of moving liquids gave me an overwhelming desire to empty my own tank! Without a bush in sight, I made use of one of the concrete pillars holding up the road above us, to gain little, if any cover from on-looking motorists as they passed. As suspected, the bike refused to start, presenting very little resistance when pressing down on the kick start lever, an attempt at bump starting it down the slight incline of the road with me pushing and Ian on the bike proved fruitless and I stopped leaving the bike rolling on ahead. We were helped by a motorist who stopped and offered his assistance.

"Have you got a tow rope?"

I shouted to the man, while trying to catch my breath. He got out of his car, opened the boot and took out a tow rope, which he attached to his tow bar while I tied the other end to the outfit. The man had left his driver's door and the tailgate open and I couldn't help notice Ian, making gestures to me with his eyes facing the top of his tilted head, he kind of nodded in the direction of the bloke's car for me to take a look. What I saw was unusual to say the least. The interior of the vehicle had been completely re-covered in a fabric that I have only seen before on a 1970's three piece suite. Seats, door panels, headlining, even the dashboard had been made to look like a tarts boudoir!

Each to their own is what I say. The man set off with Ian in hot pursuit until enough speed was achieved and the Enfield came back to life. I ran after them wearing full gear with helmet still on and jumped into the sidecar as the man unattached us, we thanked our Knight in soft velour, as he drove away and as we moved on I was glad of the speed, creating a draught as I opened my coat allowing the cool night air to surround my sweating torso.

We were again touched by the kindness of another human being, putting themselves out so that we may continue our challenge. A comforting thought.

On our way again and a little confused as to where we were, we arrived at a roundabout within the perimeters of Worthing and the engine stalled. Bollocks! Bollocks! Bollocks! I thought. We should have been here three days ago. Ian was quickly on the phone to Sam who soon arrived with his dad and a tow rope. We restarted the bike and followed them home.

Home, was a small semi detached house, somewhere in Worthing, occupied by mum and dad, Sam and his younger sister. This meant no actual room for us. We were allocated the 'Summer House' which was in fact, a shed in the back garden. The interior was the size of a double air bed, and that was what we slept on. Now, taking into account it was the middle of summer, when I say it was cold, I mean it was ffreeezing!! Never mind the snoring I think the chattering of teeth created the most noise.

As well as discussing the temperature, Ian and I spoke of the sequence of events that had made this trip very difficult. Ian came up with a theory. Although our wives had supported us when planning this trip, they weren't exactly over the moon about us disappearing out of their lives for three weeks. He suggested that between them, they had made a straw effigy of the bike and sidecar and as we disappeared into the distance through Barton on Humber, the power of voodoo came into play as they took it in turns stabbing the straw models with large pins! We laughed at the thought, but I reminded Ian of the existence of that stuffed doll hanging on the garage wall at home, and how things seem to change since it came into our lives. It felt like the inside of a fridge in that shed and I decided to put some of my clothes back on before I settled down to sleep.

A good breakfast was enjoyed the following day, after which we did what was becoming routine. We stripped the engine of the bike, revealing the cylinder head gasket was shot. Sam began searching the internet for Royal Enfield dealers anywhere close, without luck. Following another idea and after much googling he came up with a list of people in the area who were members of the Royal Enfield Owners Club. Several calls were made before Sam eventually found someone who said he may be able to help. Ian spoke to the man who didn't have a gasket but offered to make us one.

We borrowed Sam's mum's car and headed off in the direction of the address we had been given. I was the designated driver, being the only one with sufficient insurance cover, it felt slightly strange to be driving a vehicle with four road wheels and a steering wheel. I pulled on the drive at the front of a beautiful cottage, sitting back from the road in the most picturesque of settings. We were met by John, the Royal Enfield enthusiast who took us through the gate, past his house into the back garden, where the remnants of several motorcycles lay abandoned, we passed a caravan and arrived at Johns shed / workshop. Inside, the place was full of bikes, tools and machinery. It was like Aladdin's cave complete with milling machine, lathe and pillar drill. I carried with me the remains of the old gasket as a pattern. John searched through his possessions until he found a sheet of copper.09mm thick.

"Is that big enough?"

He asked. I took the piece of copper and held it against the old gasket.

"That'll do nicely."

I confirmed.

John took on the job of cutting out the large three and a half inch centre hole in the copper, using his milling machine. He left us to mark out and drill the stud holes and the two larger oil ways while he went off to make us a cuppa. Feeling at home in John's workshop Ian and I finished off the gasket by cutting around the pencil line perimeter with tin snips. We then annealed it by heating until red hot with an oxy-acetylene torch, while placed inside an old car wheel rim and leaving to cool naturally as we enjoyed our tea.

The end product was magnificent! It was a masterpiece. We thanked John and offered to pay him, to which he replied.

"Think how much it is worth to you and put it in your collection tin as a donation."

What a star!

Back at Sam's place we reassembled the bike, thinking that this must surely be the end of our troubles. We left Worthing and continued our journey along the south coast of England. We didn't get far before power was dwindling, oil leaking and our will to live was diminishing.

Arundel, a most beautiful historic town, set around its prominent castle. But it didn't seem so attractive to us, in the pouring rain when we pulled up at a hotel, only to be told.

'There was no room at the inn.'

Luckily the hotel was situated on a hill, steep enough for us to bump start the bike and find another, cheaper hotel. At the bottom of the very same hill we found one, this time Ian kept the bike running while I ran in and back out to give him the thumbs up. By now we were almost too pissed off to speak, a decision was made. Having secured a bed, we now needed a decent meal and a few pints. We sought out, discovered and enjoyed them during the course of that evening.

Thursday 8th August 7.30am. According to our original schedule, we should have woke in Newquay and be heading for Wales. Instead we were in Arundel, stripping the engine for the umpteenth time. This time though, we only removed the rocker covers before Ian spotted a problem. The inlet valve spring had broken. Via Google we found a garage listed in the town and gave them a call. The owner, Paul was very obliging, after hearing our tales of woe he suggested that we took the bike to his garage where he had a box of valve springs. He was only situated a couple of miles down the road, so we put the bike back together, loaded up our luggage and as I was expecting us to need a tow, I looked around for a suitable candidate. Meanwhile Ian gave the bike a quick try on the kick start and miraculously, it fired up!

With the engine running like a sick pig, we hobbled the bike into town where we found Enterprise Garage. Paul was another incredibly helpful bloke, who handed us a box of valve springs on arrival. We took off the cylinder head outside in the car park, and then using the workshop, with bench and vice we removed the valve. Looking through the box I realised that all of the springs were the same size, not a selection or variety of different sizes as I'd expected. After piecing together the broken spring and comparing with one from the box, guess what? It was spot on, same size! Maybe our luck was changing.

We weren't out of the water yet; we had to grind in the valve and fit the spring, and then re-fit the head. Unfortunately because of the amount of times we had taken this thing apart, some of the threads in the aluminium castings were becoming worn, in some cases even stripped. Thankfully Paul offered us the use of his Helicoil set, which we used to drill out the old threads, then re-thread the larger hole and insert steel coils which become the new thread. The only trouble with this was, because the engine was designed in the 1940's the threads were not metric and all of the inserts were. We had to improvise by using metric bolts instead of the original studs and nuts.

With all of the threads re-done, we decided to anneal the home made gasket again, in case we hadn't made it soft enough the first time. With a larger oxy-acetylene torch we heated and cooled the gasket before putting the whole thing back together.

All of this work took all of the day, we were still working on the bike after Paul had shut up shop, he wished us well and refusing to take a penny from us, he left us finishing our work in the car park.

The engine fired after a couple of kicks and a trial run up the road, told us it was more powerful than before, yet less powerful than the original engine. So we packed up and set off in the early evening. Our next stop would have been Plymouth but we simply wanted to get a few miles under our belt before finding a campsite for the night.

Heading toward Poole in Dorset and with oil now leaking so much that the rider of the bike had to wear waterproof trousers to keep the right leg dry, we found the South Lytchett Manor Caravan and Camping site. It was situated in idyllic surroundings within the grounds of the Manor House; we had stumbled on it by chance as we searched the area. The staff were very accommodating and again, there would be no charge.

If you are in a hurry, then using a classic motorcycle and sidecar as your chosen form of transport may cause you problems other than mechanical. It has a tendency to attract admirers in swarms every time you pull up, which is fine most of the time, but when it's getting late and you haven't eaten, it can be a little frustrating. After what seemed like a lifetime of answering questions from over enthusiastic onlookers, we managed to get into the site and pitch our tent.

Ian had gained information as to the location of the local watering hole and we headed off on foot. It was a long walk but the sight of the village square and the St Peters Finger pub sign in the distance was a sight for sore eyes, we walked toward it feeling like we had crossed a desert and this was our oasis.

On entering the public house, we ordered drinks and enquired about the availability of food, only to be told that the kitchens closed at 9.30 and it was now 9.38. We tried the sympathy approach, telling of our struggling, demanding charity ride but it was to no avail. Luckily, we were offered the cheese board. When I say luckily, what I mean is lucky for Ian, because he happens to love cheese, I don't!

After my meal of bread and Guinness we returned to the campsite, where we did enjoy a good night's sleep.

The following day, convinced of the need for a new head gasket, after our tea and toast breakfast, we packed up our troubles and headed toward Taunton, where we had located a Royal Enfield dealer.

At G.V. Bikes, we were met by Geoff who supplied us with the necessary gasket and allowed us to use his yard to fit it, Geoff was another good man who had a passion for Royal Enfield motorcycles and old French cars, strange as that may seem. He helped us out with the use of some tools and a cleaning solution to clean the burned oil stains from the chrome exhaust.

With the factory gasket fitted and the bike sounding pretty good, we headed back toward the south coast; passing through Exeter we arrived at Dawlish, where we searched for somewhere to stay the night. It was now the eighth day of our journey and we should have been leaving Wales, heading for Blackpool where we had another organised stop, but we had to be content with another night in the south west of England.

The Golden Sands Holiday Park was a very accommodating and very large campsite; we pitched our tent and made use of the laundry and the showers, washing both ourselves and our clothes. We left the laundry drying in the coin operated tumble driers and retired to the clubhouse. We parked the bike outside in hope of a few donations but without success, we'd had more luck earlier, outside the laundry.

Despite the enormity of the Golden Sands Holiday Park, they continued the kindness of allowing us to stay free of charge. We had a good sleep and our traditional tea and toast breakfast before continuing our journey along the coast in the direction of Lands End.

What we actually did was, we took the fastest route, which sort of followed the coast, just slightly more inland. We took the A38 for a while then the A390 taking us to Truro where we joined the A39 on to the A394 and then the A30 to Penzance. I will now try to reassure you, there will be no more listing of roads by their numbers, at least not in such quantity.

We were fast approaching the south west tip of our island and the famous tourist attraction, Lands End. During the approach it felt like we'd actually achieved something, despite all the troubles and strife's we had encountered with our three wheeled contraption, it had managed to transport us the hundreds of miles to this great landmark. We'll never know exactly how many miles, but it felt like a lot. The bike was still running and starting, it was losing power and leaking oil, but it had brought us this far on our challenge and it felt good!

We parked the bike close to the pay and display machine in the car park, however we neither paid nor displayed. A couple of quick snapshot's taken and we walked into the visitors centre, we took a look around then went into the restaurant and ordered two cream teas. We enjoyed our teas and scones with jam and clotted cream outside. The setting was idyllic and the sense of achievement somehow, warming in the cool sea breeze. It was Sunday 11th August and we agreed to make our next stop Newquay.

Get a bike it's free parking

Keith at Lands End

Ian at Lands End

Idyllic setting for cream teas

Chapter five

Our journey continued along the coast, travelling through some of the most picturesque places, on the most unique road networks in the UK. The going felt good with no time to consider how or why we had encountered so many mishaps, however they may have been brought about. The roads were barely wide enough for a single vehicle in places, winding in and out of the hills along the coast like serpents in the desert. We both agreed that this was one of the most enjoyable parts of the whole trip and we enjoyed the ride before eventually arriving at our destination. It was now evening in Newquay and we needed a campsite.

By chance, we stumbled upon what seemed like a decent sized site, with all of the necessary facilities, although despite it being the height of the tourist season, it appeared to be closed. Ian spun the bike around and as I climbed out of the sidecar a noticed a sign on the door of the reception.

> If you require assistance outside of reception hours or if you are leaving early, then please contact security on 07*********2
> Or press the red button on your right.

I pressed the button… Nothing! I dialled the number and spoke to a young lady who explained, she was the security officer. I explained our need for a place to pitch our tent and she offered us such a spot for the princely sum of £65 payable in advance. I tried to explain our situation and, as we had come to expect campsites all to be of a generous nature, pointed out how far we had travelled and not yet paid a penny to put up our tent. The lady was helpful but the decision was out of her hands and she needed to check with the management, she told me to hang up and she would be down to see us with an answer. Ian dismounted and we stretched our legs, walking around the car park and before long the security guard arrived with the news.

"I've had a word with the management and under the circumstances they are prepared to give you a discount of ten pounds."

"So, we can stay for a tenner?"

I asked, thinking that wouldn't be two bad.

"No, they'll knock a tenner off, you pay fifty five pounds."

Ian began arguing with the girl but I dragged him away, we had to make a decision, either pay, or don't stay, we didn't stay!

It didn't take long to find another, much more accommodating site, probably only a fraction of the size of the previous one, but nevertheless, a welcoming and pleasant place to park our bike. We set up camp, had a shower and enjoyed a meal in the bar, which was a big wooden shed, but such a nice shed to be in. There was no charge for the stay and we got the chance to meet more remarkable people. One person in particular greeted us in the morning with a friendly voice and showed an interest in the bike and our challenge; we spoke to him briefly before he asked.

"Have you eaten this morning?"

Having learned that we had not, the man disappeared only to return several minutes later with a plate full of hot crumpets and two mugs of tea for our breakfast, much appreciated.

We chatted as we ate, and learned that the man was living on the campsite in his caravan and going to work each day as a window cleaner, we also learned that he drove a jeep, which is a handy thing to know if you may need a tow, and we did. With everything packed away the window cleaner gave us a tow and with the bike running we didn't get the chance to thank the most helpful gentleman, nor did we learn his name. In fear of stalling the engine we left with merely a thankful wave.

The relationship between motorcycle and sidecar is a strange one. The motorcycle was designed and developed as a two wheeled vehicle, steered when in motion by leaning one way or the other. The more you lean, the tighter you turn. When you attach a sidecar to the bike you prevent it from leaning and the only way to steer is by using the handlebars. This is the reason some people claim that you cannot ride a combination, you have to drive it. Now putting together the bike and sidecar does not make it simply a three wheeler like the Reliant Robin, because the wheels do not form a symmetrical triangle. When setting up the alignment of the combination you have to make the sidecar tow in toward the bike, while also making the bike lean out, away from the sidecar. All of this is done by trial and error as it is not an exact science, however when done correctly, this wonky set up should drive as if it were meant to be together, which it never was. The mounting brackets holding the thing together need to be strong as the sidecar will be longing to travel in a different direction to the bike.

This next section of our journey, with its winding roads and steep inclines began to take its toll on the outfit and there seemed to be some flexing between bike and sidecar on the tight bends. The ride itself, whether on the bike or in the sidecar was an exhilarating one, similar to a roller coaster and it was fun! We travelled for miles on these roads until; on one piece of road we ascended a steep incline and then, as we went into a right hand hairpin bend, with me in the sidecar, SNAP! The outfit sank in the middle and Ian pulled up. Luckily we were travelling at low speed for the bend as the front lower bracket had broken and the rear lower one had torn almost through. Ian let the sickened machine roll gently backward down the hill to a point where right on the bend was a pull in, he then slowly edged us forward, taking us off the main road and we both dismounted.

The area was large enough for, maybe three or four small cars, we were surrounded by woodland and to our right was a gate, beyond the gate was a skip full of old broken up kitchen units and the other side of the skip were piles of building materials. It seemed a strange and isolated place for a builder's yard. I inspected the damage and removed the front bracket, it was the smallest of the four mounting points and I figured I may be able to repair it. The rear one would be a little trickier as it needed some welding. Ian pointed out that we had recently passed a pub and he decided to go and seek help. I looked over the gate at the skip and its contents, wondering if any of the old units might still have the steel angle brackets attached to them, used for securing to the wall. I was about to climb over the gate when a pickup truck arrived, stopping at the gate. Three men sat in a row across the cab of the truck. I stepped back from the gate and moved toward the bike. The men got out of the cab, one went to open the gate and the other two came toward me. I picked up the broken bracket and explained.

"Were in a bit of a pickle, this brackets broken and I need a bit of steel to fix it."

"I doubt if we've got anything."

One of them replied.

"What about the skip, maybe a bracket or something?"

I suggested, and the two men went to speak with their colleague. They shouted back to me.

"You can have a look if you like."

That was all I needed to hear, I was in that skip like a rat up a drainpipe. I was confident there would be something in there. As I rummaged the men unloaded the pickup, throwing more stuff into the skip. Then I found it! Exactly what I'd been looking for, a piece of chipboard that would have started out life as a base unit, and still screwed to it were two steel angle brackets. I removed them and returned to where the bike was parked and using a stone for my anvil, I knocked the brackets into the shape I required. The trouble now was, I had forgotten one important part of the operation, the bit that needed a drill! Returning to the workmen I asked, without much hope and they replied by shaking their heads, suddenly one of the men pointed to the sky and with a promising smile on his face, he went to the pickup. From under the passenger seat he revealed a battery powered drill in a plastic case with a selection of drill bits. I drilled the necessary holes and with nuts and bolts from my miscellaneous nut and bolt container, I fastened the bracket together and fitted it back on the bike.

Ian returned to explain that he had met a man in the pub who knew a man who owned a garage in the town close by. I told him of my repair job and we agreed that while it would enable us to move the bike, it really did need some welding on the rear bracket. We packed away the tools and thanking the very helpful workmen, we travelled back down the hill to the pub, where we enjoyed our lunch and the man who knew a man offered to take us to him. We finished our sandwich while the man finished his pint, which I am sure was not the only pint he had consumed during his time at the bar. We left the pub and Ian got on the bike whereas I joined the man in his car, we led the way and Ian followed.

Granville Garages Exmoor

Granville Garages, Exmoor was where we had arrived and we took off both lower brackets. The man, who had brought us, went off to his shop somewhere in the town, leaving us with the man he knew, who was a very helpful man, he welded our brackets and supplied us with some paint to slap on after they had cooled. We refitted them and prepared to leave. At this point the original man returned with a carrier bag full of pies, sandwiches, pasties and crisps for our journey. We thanked them both, neither of them would accept any payment from us and once again, we were back on the road.

The sidecar seemed sufficiently secured as we continued our journey but the bike was struggling and we desperately needed to get to Bristol. I had spoken to Henry, the man who had an engine with no cylinder head, I had phoned while in Clacton. He now invited us to call at his place and he had given us his post code.

Ian had an app on his phone that resembled something to do with satellite navigation, although it did tend to lose signal quite frequently as well as having a delayed action, which could prove very frustrating. Conversation went something like this with me on the bike and Ian in the chair…

Ian – "Turn left at these lights."
Keith – "These lights?"
Ian – "No!... Why did you turn left?"
Keith – "You told me to."
Ian – "Not these lights, I meant the next set."
Keith – "Ok, I'll turn around… Left here then?"
Ian – "No! Why did you turn left?"
Keith – "Because you said, the next set of lights."
Ian – "It's saying the one after the roundabout."
Keith – "I'll turn around."
Ian – "Go straight on at the roundabout."
Keith – "There are some light coming up. Left here?"
Ian – "I've lost the signal.. Fuck it, go straight on!"
Keith – "We've come too far, this is the wrong village!"
Ian – "I've got it now; we should have turned left at that first

set of lights!"
We did eventually find our way, or at least found our way to
where Ian's phone declared.
"You have arrived at your destination."

Henry's place

We pulled into a farm yard that resembled an army base. It was full of ex- military vehicles, including tanks, armoured cars, jeeps and even gun trailers. All of them were painted in sand coloured camouflage. It was as if they had just returned from Afghanistan. A man came out to us and when we explained our real destination, he told us with a smile that it was the other side of his farm. He directed us, across the farm as a short cut, which led us to Henry's place. We chugged onto the drive where the engine stalled in a cloud of smoke, as if it were saying.

"That's it lads, I've had enough."

Henry came out to welcome us; he lived in a detached house on a country lane where there was no evidence of neighbours in any direction. The house stood close to the lane in a beautifully mature and cared for garden. At the end of the drive was Henry's garage, which had an extension on the side, used as an office. He showed us around. The front half of the garage, with its double doors housed several Royal Enfield motorcycles, some of them fitted with diesel engines. The bikes were surrounded by shelves, well stocked with spare parts. Henry's own motorbike stood on the drive.

First things first! We needed somewhere to stay as it was now late afternoon, we enquired about campsites in the area, to which Henry replied in his strong South Gloucestershire accent.

"No need, you can stay 'ere, put your tent up at the bottom of our garden, by that willow tree."

He pointed out the position as he continued.

"We'll 'ave some dinner an' I'll get us some beers. We can sort the bike out tomorrow,"

His accent made him sound like a friendly pirate. We unpacked the bike and pitched the tent while Henry took off in his car to fetch some beers. Dinner was cooked by Henry's wife, a delicious chilli, enjoyed outdoors in the warm summer evening, accompanied by cold bottled beers.

The following morning, we ate a cooked breakfast outside, before the inevitable stripping of the engine. This time we fitted a new piston and rings, the old rings appeared to be seized into the piston which would explain the lack of compression and the build up of back pressure, causing the oil to leak out and the gaskets to blow. Henry ground the cylinder head against the barrel to ensure a good flat surface. While doing this he noticed that the inlet valve was regressed, it had sunk into the head, a problem we had no way of solving as Henry didn't have a replacement head. We fitted another new head gasket and reassembled the engine. It was time to move on.

Henry accompanied us on his motorcycle, he lead us across the Severn Bridge and into Wales, but the engine was pinking, indicating a timing issue. After travelling a suitable distance past the bridge and away from traffic, Henry pulled into the gateway to, what looked like a park. It had a gatehouse behind a pair of large wrought iron gates and a stone perimeter wall.

Henry adjusted the timing and noticing a leak from the exterior oil pipe, he attempted to tighten it, unfortunately it snapped!

"Not to worry, I'll nip back an' fetch one."

He said cheerily as he jumped on his bike and disappeared in the direction of the bridge.

There we were, stuck at the side of the road, again! There was nothing we could do at this point except reflect on the disastrous journey we had travelled over the past ten days. It was now Tuesday 13th August and we should have been arriving in Scotland, whereas we had only just touched Wales. We simply dealt with each problem as it arrived and moved on, it's only when you're stuck with time on your hands that you start to question, why? We did just that and found no answers as we both drifted off to sleep, lying on the stone wall basking in the afternoon sun.

The thunderous roar of Henry's 535cc Bullet brought us back to consciousness. Henry quickly fitted the oil pipe; we thanked him for all his help and set off across South Wales. The bike appeared to be running ok and we soon clocked up a few miles, passing through Swansea we continued along the coastal road. I was in the saddle and with all thoughts of voodoo and the like far from away from us, never had there been two people more determined to put the past behind them and enjoy the ride from here on in.

While passing through a seaside town in the deep south of

Wales, I pulled up at a set of lights, glancing to my right I noticed something in an antiques shop window. The back of the window display opened like a door and a hand reached in and grabbed, by the scruff of the neck something that resembled someone, I did not want reminding of. I stopped the bike at the far side of the lights and shouted to Ian,

"Did you see that!?"

"See what?"

He asked as he took off his helmet.

"That dummy in the shop window, it was the spitting image of that thing I found in the sidecar!"

Ian got out of the sidecar.

"I need to stretch my legs."

He said casually, before crossing the road. He walked back to the shop and looked in the window, he returned and while squeezing himself back into the tight space, he shook his head saying.

"You're becoming paranoid!"

I didn't even bother to explain, the bike was still running, so I clicked it into gear and carried on. We continued along the coast to a place called the Mumbles, on the western edge of Swansea bay, it felt like an isolated place, although there was a large car park that edged onto some cliffs and as we drew alongside the entrance to the car park, the bike, which had been running like a top let out a noise that we had become accustomed to. The familiar sound was that of exhaust gases escaping through a hole in the cylinder head gasket. I turned into the car park and stopped the engine. We sat for a moment, staring from the cliff top out to sea, which was a distance below us. I made a suggestion.

"Why don't we pour the spare can of petrol over the bike, set it alight and push the fuckin' thing over the cliff into the sea? We could video it, using our phones and put it on Utube. We might even make some money out of it for the charity."

Ian thought for a moment and admitted.

"It's tempting!"

I removed myself from the bike, taking a few deep breaths as I walked way. Ian got out of the sidecar. It would be something of an understatement to mention at this point, that our spirits were lower than a snake's belly.

Chapter six

Certain things had to be taken into consideration before taking on this challenge. During the recovery period, after my time in hospital, I was referred to a Hypo Unawareness team at my local hospital. The team had been set up to help people like me, who had suffered serious hypos. It was led by a professor and included a doctor, a specialist diabetes nurse, a dietician and a psychologist.

I was having trouble getting to sleep, out of fear that I may not wake in the morning and the team were worried that I may have lost the early warning signs that usually help to identify an oncoming hypo. These signs can be things like, sweating, trembling, hunger, tiredness, fatigue and confusion along with many more and recognising one, or a combination of some of these symptoms, enables us to eat or drink something sweet to restore glucose levels in the blood, therefore avoiding episodes similar to my experience in 2009. After living with diabetes for as many years as I have, your body can become used to lower levels of glucose and the symptoms can disappear, making life a little dangerous and because these changes happen over a period of time, they can go unnoticed.

The team helped me in many ways, I spent a lot of time with the psychologist who helped me to understand why I was thinking the way I was. I spent time with the nurse, who helped me with the management of my diabetes, encouraging me to accept higher blood glucose levels and therefore regaining some of the warning signs. I also spent time with the doctor who suggested I try out a new device. A continuous blood glucose monitor. Up until this point, to measure your blood glucose levels, you had to do a test involving pricking you finger and applying a small amount of blood onto a test strip that goes into a meter which, after a few seconds gives you a digital read out of your glucose level, in short known as a BG test. The continuous glucose meter picks up a signal from a transmitter that takes information from a small sensor piercing the skin on your arm or abdomen. Each sensor is applied by attaching a holder that uses adhesive tape to secure it to your skin, you then have a pre loaded device to fire the sensor into the skin and after attaching the transmitter to the holder you have five days sensor life before you have to relocate and repeat the process. The receiver has many functions which include alarms to inform you of a low or a high BG and can even predict a fall or rise in blood glucose.

I can honestly say, since receiving and using my continuous glucose meter, I have never looked back. It has changed my life completely and I am sure that without it, I would not have been able to take on this challenge, Ian would not have been so willing to join me and I'm pretty certain that Lucy would never have agreed to it.

So, with the perfect partnership it was made possible. As I rode the bike, Ian had the meter in its holder on the dash of the sidecar and in the event of a projected low BG I could be forewarned and swap from rider to passenger until my sugar levels had sufficiently risen, usually with the help of jelly babies, always kept to hand.

I also had to deal with the pain from the several fractured vertebrae which although now healed, still cause me considerable discomfort. More importantly I had to consider the possibility of further fractured bones, while bouncing about in plywood box fastened to the side of a motorbike. Each time a pot hole is hit while sitting in the sidecar, as your bum leaves the seat you hold your breath and hope that you will survive the landing.

I've taken the time to mention these things in order to help you understand how I didn't make the decision to do this trip lightly, to understand the importance of completing it and how ultimately, failure was not an option!

Having contemplated for a while, considering and eventually deciding, we did what we do best. We rolled up our sleeves and got out the tools. We were joined in the car park by people who seemed to pull up alongside, watch us work for a while and then leave.

Although some decided to stay and watch with intensity, while drinking tea from a flask and eating sandwiches, two brothers, at their wits end, stripping and rebuilding what was proving to be the most unreliable machine ever known to man.

We fitted the new gasket supplied by Henry and after putting it all back together; the engine started and ran as it should. We packed everything away and left the car park via the entrance, instead of the considered option, via the sea!

I continued to ride and instinctively turned left as we rode out of the car park, ensuring I thought, that we would be continuing along the coast line. Somehow, things didn't work out that way and after endlessly riding around a large housing estate, I stopped! We argued! I rode on, I stopped! We argued! I rode on, after what seemed like an eternity of this we ended up on a familiar road, familiar because it was the road we had used to enter into this god forsaken hole! We were somehow back at the Swansea end of the peninsular and now, keeping left was the right thing to do. It steered us into the direction we should have been travelling.

We arrived at a town named Llanelli, it was late and it was raining, we were exhausted, wet and in need of a bed with a roof. In the centre of the town we discovered a Travelodge, we booked in and learned that the 'restaurant' was a pub around the corner owned by the hotel. After a shower and shave, we discussed our next move over dinner and a pint.

Taking into consideration, everything we had been through, and agreeing that the engine would probably not manage to take us the remainder of our journey, we hatched a plan. We would head for Cheadle, where we had purchased the engine and see if we could get any help from John.

During our very brief stay, we learned that Llanelli was famous for the Stepney Spare Wheel. A universal, spokeless wheel invented in 1904 for motor vehicles which, at the time were manufactured without a spare wheel. In 1909 it was boasted that every London Taxi had a Stepney Spare Wheel fitted. A fairly useless piece of information, I know but, I thought it worthy of a mention.

The following day we telephoned John who agreed to help as

best he could. It was another rainy day in Wales; we retightened the head bolts after breakfast in the pub, loaded up our luggage and headed for the hills, or was it the valleys? Probably both. The rain soon eased as we crossed Wales, now avoiding the coast and heading directly for Wrexham in the north east, close to the border.

The engine was now leaking oil again, out of every gap it could find its way out of, whoever rode the bike had the. 'Oil soaked right leg syndrome.' In Ian's case, slightly worse as his waterproof trousers now had a hole below the right knee, where he had burned them on the exhaust, allowing the oil to soak into his jeans and the inside of his boot. We had very little compression and starting the bike was becoming more and more difficult.

Travelling through Wrexham, on a straight flat road we hit traffic, quite a congestion and we were stop starting along the road, Ian was on the bike and as the traffic began moving, he set off, probably travelling further than we had for a long time when the van in front of us stopped dead! We didn't! Ian had taken his eye off the road for a second and we were heading for the rear of a large white van. I shouted as loud as my lungs would allow me WHOA!!! Ian hit the brakes and we came to an almost immediate stop with the front tyre of the bike millimetres from the vans rear bumper and with the front springs coil bound for a millisecond before recoiling to their original position causing the front of the outfit to react like an untamed stallion. All of this happened in a flash, the engine stalled and with only a moment to catch our breath, we had to get the bike running again. A couple of attempts on the kick start proved fruitless, so we now had to get the machine out of the line of traffic.

This long straight road seemed to be without side streets, to our left was a row of buildings almost touching the road and to our right I noticed a large entrance to something or other. We quickly dismounted and pushed the outfit across the road, dodging oncoming traffic as best we could. We entered the driveway of somewhere quite grand, a pair of stone pillars either side of the entrance to... We looked beyond the walls that led out from the pillars and saw a hill, but not just any old hill. The ground rose up, revealing well kept grass with paths travelling up and down, beautiful spreads of floral borders with bouquets of colour bursting out across the peaceful, calm landscape.

The hillside was a graveyard, and the only incline suitably steep enough for us to bump start the bike. We had no option; we pushed the fully loaded combination onto the hallowed ground and up the central path. After a long slow push, we paused for breath and admired the view, mainly gravestones. We also took the opportunity to discuss peoples possible opinions on what we were doing, mainly the residents. Our reckoning was, some would think we lacked any respect for the dead, while a few of them would likely give us a smile and I'm sure at least a couple would have given us a push and of course, if Charlie had been with us, he could have asked them! The bike started and we thanked and apologised to the residents before continuing on our way.

Fuel stops were frequent and we were now at the point where we had to look for petrol stations situated on a hill, so we could bump start the bike. On some occasions, when a suitable incline was not available we actually filled the tank with the engine running. Not an advisable thing to do and please do not try this at home! We did run out of fuel at one point, we found ourselves in Queensferry somehow and as we rode through the town centre, looking for a suitable petrol station, with the bike running on reserve tank, the engine stopped. Luckily we turned off the main road and onto a side road with a suitable incline. We free wheeled onto a wide pavement where we emptied the spare can of fuel into the tank.

It was a warm afternoon and the streets were busy, we had a lot of admirers stop and talk to us, (admiring the bike, not us personally) when a Land Rover pulled up alongside us. The window wound down and a man shouted to us, above the noise of the traffic and the admiring public.

"Are you alright, do you need any help?"

"No, thanks but were out of petrol and I have some here."

I shouted back, I left Ian to deal with the bike and walked toward the Land Rover.

"Will it start ok?"

The man asked, I explained that we may have to bump start it and as he seemed interested I went on to explain our need to get to Cheadle for a replacement engine. I have to say that the man's response took me by surprise; in fact I was overwhelmed as the man offered to put us up at a pub he owned locally, he also offered to send someone with a truck to pick up the engine and the use of a garage at the pub to work on the bike. How amazing is that from complete stranger?

Ian, having finished the refuelling, had joined me at the Land Rover and the two of us thanked the man for his generous offer, however we insisted that we carried on as best we could. We did suggest that he waited until the bike was running, before leaving, in case we needed a tow, the man agreed. We walked back to the bike and pushed it onto the road, as we were about to begin the downhill push, a woman stopped and asked if she could help, I said.

"We could do with a push."

She appeared to be in the company of a teenage girl, probably her daughter. The woman answered.

"No problem."

She turned around and beckoned to a teenage lad, who had been walking several paces behind them.

"Oi! Come 'ere an' give these a push."

The teenager lifted his eyes up from his phone and strolled across to us with a look on his face that said.

"Thank's a lot mum!"

With the help of the young man, we pushed the bike downhill; I jumped aboard and clicked it into gear. As I let out the clutch the engine fired up and I spun the bike around, I picked up Ian, we thanked the young man, as well as the guy in the Land Rover and with a wave to the helpful mum, we were on our way, yet again.

I have already and will continue to mention, the incredibly helpful people we encountered on our journey, this was no exception, we seemed, somehow, to bring out the good in people and it continued with us throughout our journey.

Our next stop had to be petrol, preferably on a hill. We travelled in the rough direction we thought to be the way we should be going, unfortunately no hills! The further we travelled the more desperate we became and with non spare, running out of fuel was not an option. The site of a large petrol station ahead was too much, I pulled in, we refuelled and ate the remains of the carrier bag of pasties we had carried with us. A slight incline tempted us to give bump starting a try, without success. We paused for breath in the middle of the road, which appeared to lead onto a housing estate, when we were assaulted by the loudest female voice I have heard in a long while.

"Hey up, it's Wallace and Grommet!"

The voice, which was enhanced by a strong Liverpuddlion accent, came from a head hanging out of a 4x4 vehicle which suddenly stopped and reversed to our side.

"Do you's need any 'elp?"

We were asked by a woman who's bright red head of hair was as loud as her voice.

"We could do with a tow."

Ian answered, the scary woman replied, explaining.

"I'm on me way out now, but I'll get you's a tow."

She drove forward, turning the vehicle around and then drove past us, back onto the estate.

"What was that?"

Ian asked, looking at me in expectation of an answer.

"I haven't got the foggiest idea!"

I shook my head in disbelief and while trying to work out our next move, the 4x4 returned.

"He's on 'is way with a tow rope, what's up wi' it anyway?"

The lady asked.

"The engines about knackered, were on our way to get another one."

I explained. She laughed, loudly and said.

"Serves you right for riding an Indian Enfield, I'm a biker, so is he, I've told 'im Wallace and Grommet 'ave broke down at the end of the road. Ha ha ha, I've gorra go, he'll sort you out."

With that she left and before we had chance to comment, a car pulled up and the male driver shouted to us.

"She told me Wallace and Grommet needed a tow, I see what she fuckin' meant now! Where are you goin' lads?"

I explained our original challenge and how we were now heading for Cheadle, the man told us he too had diabetes and was on his way to hospital for his eye screening appointment, when his wife had stopped and ordered him to help us out. He turned his car around and stopped in front of the bike. He produced a tow rope from the boot which we fastened to the bike and his tow bar. Ian sat on the bike and before long the single cylinder engine burst into life, but not for long. Ian spun the bike around and after thanking the man we attempted to ride off into the sunset when that, oh so familiar sound appeared. The phut phut phutting of exhaust gases escaping through the side of the engine, yes. The cylinder head gasket had blown itself to pieces, again!

Each blow we received, usually in the form of our motorcycle attempting to self destruct, had a devastating effect on our moral, yet with every disaster came a glimmer of hope, almost always in the shape of incredibly kind people.

Dave, the man with the loud wife was still with us, he pulled his car in front of the bike and gave us a few comforting words.

"Don't worry lad's, we'll get this sorted, I'm gonna give you a tow to our 'ouse, it's just around the corner, I've gorra get to my appointment but it won't take long."

He attached the rope to our bike and towed us to his house on a cul-de-sac within the modern housing estate. We pushed the outfit onto the front garden and Dave asked if we needed anything.

"Only a head gasket."

I said as we prepared to strip the bike.

"Don't worry, I'll sort that for you, I've gorra go now lad's I'm late,"

He jumped in his car and drove away.

As I write this, I'm thinking... To a reader this must seem strange. Two brothers with a determination to travel the circumference of mainland Britain, on what must seem like the most ridiculous form of transport end up on a front garden, belonging to an eccentric couple from Liverpool at a place they don't even know the name of and they are left there, by someone they have never met before to begin stripping the engine. At the time, it seemed surreal, it must seem that way as you read it, why? Because it was!

We had no time to wonder how we had ended up there; it was now the afternoon of Wednesday 14th August, which happened to be Ian's birthday, a time we had planned to celebrate in Bonnie Scotland. Instead we had to fix the bike and get ourselves inland to Cheadle. As we worked on the bike in the heat of the day, Jan, the fiery haired woman returned home, loudly! She took the time to introduce herself and tell us that she and Dave were bikers, who knew people who would help. She went into the house and released the most enormous dog onto the front. It was a Weimaraner, a breed I had never heard of, it looked like a large Doberman with the colouring of a Great Dane and luckily, a very placid temperament.

Jan told us of her and Dave's time spent in India, riding hired Royal Enfield's and of Dave's passion for Harley Davidson's. I told her of our need for a head gasket and she got on the phone to a colleague, asking if they could help. The conversation was short, after which Jan announced, in a trivial manner.

"He's on his way with a gasket for you."

The ease in which she had found a gasket led me to recall the times we had searched, travelled for and even hand made a 500cc Bullet head gasket. I soon returned to reality with an urgent need to 'spend a penny.' I asked Jan.

"Could I use your toilet?"

For the first time since we had met, Jan became silent, she stared into my eyes and I watched as the colour drained from her face. It was as if I had asked to move in with them. After a silent pause, she spoke quietly, with fear in her voice.

"You'll 'ave to take your boots off! I don't mind in the kitchen, but the rest o' the 'ouse.. And don't touch anything!"

I followed Jan into the house, after removing my boots at the door. In the kitchen, Jan opened the door to the living room and gave me directions to the upstairs bathroom. As I reached the door,

Jan stopped me and attempted to explain.

"Everything 'as to be in its place, I'm alright in the kitchen but everywhere else... Do you understand?"

I felt she needed me to understand and told her.

"Of course I do, don't worry, I only want a wee."

I entered the living room which was spotless, like a dressed show house, the stairs and landing were equally clean and un-cluttered and the bathroom had not a bottle out of place, everything lined up symmetrically. I used the loo, carefully, I then washed my hands, but the black oil mixed with soap began to splash grey dots on the brilliant white porcelain and then on the tiles, I moved my hands in panic causing them to drip onto the floor! Aaargh! What could I do? I quickly rinsed my hands under the tap and using toilet roll; I traced my steps and cleaned every drip, continuing until highly polished. I went to the towel to wipe my hands but after looking at the precision in which it had been placed, I wiped my hands on my shirt and hurried back downstairs. I entered the kitchen expecting Jan to be standing there holding a meat cleaver in a threatening pose. But the room was empty, I left the house, replaced my boots and joined Ian, Jan and the dog outside, where normality had returned, Jan was as loud as ever as she talked with Ian and we were soon joined by Dave returned from his eye screening appointment.

With all the necessary bolts undone, we tried to remove the cylinder head but it needed a little gentle persuasion, unfortunately I had left our hammer at the side of the road when the sidecar broke loose in Exmoor National Park. I asked Dave if we might borrow one, slightly unsure of his response.

"Hey lad, come with me."

He led me through the rear garden into his workshop where, undergoing a custom rebuild was the most beautiful Harley Davidson sat on stands being hand crafted into something very special.

"I'm waitin' for delivery of some stainless steel for it."

He explained as I drooled over the machine. Dave opened a drawer containing a selection of hammers and said.

"Here y'are lad, take your pick, ha ha or should I say take your hammer, hey?"

I chose a hammer similar to the one I had lost, one with a yellow handle and I have no idea why. We returned to the garden where, using the hammer I tapped off the cylinder head. We were joined by a man who looked like a long haired greasy biker. That's not an insult by the way; he worked with motorcycles and had long hair. How else would he look? He carried with him just what we needed, another head gasket!

We only had to travel eighty miles to get to John's place and I suppose we would have done anything to get there, however I never thought we would end up doing what we did. The man with the gasket joined us closely as we examined the damage to the existing gasket. After a long discussion, informing him of the history of the mechanics of our journey, he suggested we dismiss all thoughts of using a head gasket and simply refit the head without a gasket. We considered his theory and decided to do just that, after all if there were no gasket, what could blow?

We rebuilt the engine, the greasy biker left us with the gasket, at no charge and we left Dave and Jan's house after thanking them over and over, they responded by saying, in that wonderful Liverpool accent.

"We're bikers, we've gorra stick together."

Ian and I left that cul-de-sac with a warm feeling of genuine niceness and headed for Cheadle. We travelled the miles, mostly with oil pumping from the engine onto the right leg until Ian suggested we remove the oil filler cap. Eureka! The oil was being forced out of the engine by crankcase compression, with the oil filler cap removed the pressure left via the filler neck and with rag wrapped around it we suppressed the flow of oil onto our leg.

We arrived at John's place and having been there before; we knew that parking was an issue. We pulled onto the pavement opposite his house, which was positioned on a very busy road with very few gaps in the flow of traffic. Crossing the road was like dicing with death as the endless rush of traffic sped past; reaching the other side in one piece seemed like a major achievement.

Having reached the other side we went into John's place and as we crossed the yard, we were met by John who appeared from his workshop saying.

"I've just been speaking to someone who knows you two."
Who?
I asked, puzzled as to who this person could possibly have been.
John went on to explain.

"I phoned a friend of mine about an engine I have and he used to own. Henry, down near Bristol, he said you stayed at his place."

It seemed, anyone involved with Royal Enfield's knows Henry. The good thing for us about this was, Henry had confirmed everything we had said about the engine we bought from John, basically that it was knackered. This appeared to have made John seem a little more charitable and he agreed to replace it with the one he had removed from a bike formerly belonging to Henry. It was one that in the past, Henry had rebuilt and upgraded to 535cc and John had hoped to use for a trials bike he intended to build for himself.

Having been fed all this information and with the knowledge we would be fitting another, better, more powerful engine the following day, our moral was lifted above gutter level and we decided to find somewhere to stay the night. John made a call to the Kings Head, a public house at the bottom of the hill, things were looking up. We removed our luggage and John gave us a lift down the road.

Inside, we were shown to our room by Daisy, one of the bar staff. After a shower etc we returned to the bar where we enjoyed the first of many drinks to come, after all it was my brother's birthday. We were joined later by John and we enjoyed a meal together, after which John left us and we spent the rest of the evening in the bar, where Daisy kept us amused with tales of her beloved Morris Minor and her hot and cold relationship with her older lover!

The next day, after enjoying a cooked breakfast, we packed our stuff into the panniers and decided to walk the short distance up the hill back to John's place. We soon realised that the 'short distance' in a car can be quite a distance on foot and with the weight of the

Leather pannier full of clothes, our short walk seem like another desert crossing.

After a short rest and a quick cup of tea, we removed the engine from the bike and fitted the new 535cc. We did this in John's back yard and it was a few hours before we were ready to kick it up. While there, we acquired from John a speedometer with a working odometer, unfortunately it was in Kilometres, we also replaced the rear light again along with one or two other minor details, before the moment of truth.

Ignition on, petrol on, slowly turn the engine over using the kick start lever until it reaches top dead centre and the ammeter shows a discharge, pull in the decompression lever and with all your weight, push down on the kick start, while releasing the decompression lever and the damn thing should burst into life, and guess what?.. It did! A few minor adjustments, mainly the carburettor and we were cooking on gas. We thanked John and set off to resume our position on the coast. Our next destination was one we had pre-arranged, close to Blackpool where we should have been four days ago.

Chapter seven

During the previous summer we attended many shows and summer fairs, usually by prior booking through the organisers. As one particular week in August drew close, Lucy pointed out to me that it was the week of the Bakewell Show. The show is an enormous agricultural extravaganza, with Shire horses, sheep. Cows and the like, stalls and fun fair rides and food of all types along with, most importantly a classic car and bike show. As it was too late to book in, on the Wednesday I decided to take the outfit for a ride out to Bakewell which is situated only twenty miles from our home. The traffic was horrendous but I eventually reached Bakewell where I headed for the showground. Parking at these events can be a nightmare, but I figured I could squeeze the bike in somewhere without getting a parking ticket. I followed the signs for the car parks but became impatient and decided to turn onto one of the lanes. As I did this a young man wearing a hi-vis waistcoat waved me toward him. I followed his instruction which involved guiding me onto another lane where I came across another bright yellow waistcoat, he held up his hand for me to stop, I did as the young man moved to one side and opened a gate into a field, waving me through, as I passed him he said.

"Park it on the right there mate, with the others."

I acknowledged with a wave and rode into the show ground right among the classic car and bike show.

What could I do, but pretend I was supposed to be there? I positioned the bike and presented a donation bucket from the boot. Interest was good and money came my way, when a lady approached me asking.

"Could I offer you a bed for the night?"

I was surprised by the question and gave my answer instinctively.

"You're a bit forward aren't you? We've only just met."

The lady replied with.

If you're travelling around the coast of Britain, then you'll be passing through Blackpool, we live in Blackpool and can offer you a bed, a meal, a shower and I'll do your laundry."

I didn't have to think for long before I replied.

"That is a very kind offer and we may just take you up on it."

Introducing themselves as Kath and her husband Andy, they left us with a card. Almost one year later, once we had worked out a schedule, I gave them a call. I spoke to Andy and after explaining who I was, the bloke with the motorbike and sidecar at the Bakewell Show. I told him we should be close to Blackpool on the 11th August. Andy said they would be looking forward to our arrival.

It was now the 15th and we were in Stoke on Trent, trying desperately to get out, the M6 motorway was at a standstill and every road we took seemed to bring us back to the motorway. The bike was running good with loads more power than before, although there was a lot of vibration from the engine. A close inspection revealed one of the bolts holding an anti vibration bracket was missing, probably not tightened after the engine fit. We called at a garage and begged a bolt; the kind gentleman gave us two, one for a spare. We fitted the bolt which reduced the vibration and decided we would have to take the motorway if we were to have any hope of getting out of here.

We kept Andy and Kath informed of our progress via text and they were now expecting us later that day. We joined the M6 and eventually passed the backlog of traffic. No problem now, we were flying. Previously we had avoided the motorway because we couldn't keep up with the flow of traffic, but we were cruising now, I was in the saddle and enjoying the new found power, thinking to myself, this is how it should have been from the start when it started to rain, I don't mean a quick shower, It began to piss it down, and continued to come down in buckets for the rest of the day.

As we arrived in Blackpool in the late afternoon we found the address on the outskirts relatively easy. After the battering from the torrential rain, the sight of the double garage door opening as we pulled on the drive was a welcomed one. Andy instructed us to pull into the garage. We dismounted, dripping wet, soaked through to the skin in places and cold. We took off our outer layers, jacket and trousers, which were no longer waterproof as I too had burned a hole in mine.

The inside of the garage resembled a Chinese laundry by the time we had finished hanging up our wet clothes to dry. Andy showed us to our rooms, yes one each! We took our luggage and had a shower. With dry clothes on we joined Andy in the living room who welcomed us with a cold beer apiece, hmmm.

Considering we were in the house of a relative stranger, we felt at home. It was a lovely house and they were lovely people, although Kath was still at work at this point. She had left Andy in charge of preparing an evening meal, meat and potato pie, hmmm. Andy didn't seem too confident in the kitchen, but became more relaxed after a few bottles of beer. We learned a little about their lives and told of our experiences on this incredible journey. Andy kept referring to his written instructions with regards to the cooking, Ian made a suggestion.

"I think you should probably check the oven now."

Andy referred to his instructions and disagreed.

"No, its fine for another ten minutes, it says so here."

Ian replied.

"It doesn't smell fine mate, it smells like it's burning to me."

Andy jumped to his feet and ran into the kitchen in a panic.

Despite a slightly burned crust the meal was delicious, finished off competently by Kath on her return, who fulfilled her promise of washing our clothes, what a star.

Overall we had a comfortable, relaxing evening, which we were in need of to recharge our batteries. With an excellent night's sleep in a room on our own; followed by a cooked breakfast in the morning. We loaded up our clean dry clothes and headed north with confidence.

Passing through Morecambe and Lancaster we were heading for Carlisle when we hit road works, in fact the whole road was being resurfaced and had traffic lights set up frequently along the road. The tail backs were enormous and we were moving at a snail's pace. Ordinarily, this can be frustrating, but when you are as far behind schedule on your road trip as we were... If either of us had hair we would have been pulling it out by now! For the first time in the two weeks we had been travelling, the bike was running like a Swiss gold lever watch and here we were, sitting in a line of traffic for what seemed like hours, on a sunny day in August, which is not an insignificant piece of information. When riding a motorcycle, even in warm weather, suitable clothing is required to keep you warm as you ride, however when not moving and the sun is shining it can become a little too hot, in your helmet, gloves and coat, in fact before long you begin sweating like a turkey two days before Christmas! We decided to turn off the main road at the next available opportunity. Slowly, on our right hand side a road came into view and as we drew closer to it, Ian pulled the bike out of the line of traffic and rode along the wrong side of the road until we reached the turn off, he turned right and at last we were free!

The road we had taken was no more than a single track, we had to slow down to an almost stop to allow oncoming cyclists to pass. We encountered steep inclines, tight bends and dead ends where we were forced to turn around. We turned left and then right and then left and... yes we were lost! Each side of the roads were high hedges, it was as if we were in a maze on a motorcycle and sidecar combination. I remembered my time as a young boy in the scouts. If you were lost and without a compass, use the sun as your guide to work out the direction you need to travel. Ian pulled up at a cross roads. Now, we knew we needed to go north, and the sun rises in the east and sets in the west. All we had to was work out the position of the sun, take into consideration the time of day and Bob's your uncle.

"What time is it?"

I asked Ian.

"Twelve o'clock, nearly dinner time."

He answered rubbing his belly.

"Where's the sun?"

I asked.

"There."

Ian replied pointing straight up to the sky.

"Which way did it come up?"

I asked.

"How the fuck do I know, I was riding the fuckin' bike."

Ian answered politely.

"Oh bollocks to it, turn right."

I instructed, and Ian did just that. After several more turns, both left and right, we saw a sign post listing a number of A roads in the direction of a narrow uphill road. We followed the sign and at the top of the hill was indeed a long straight A road, full of standing traffic.

After approximately one hour of driving around an enormous maze, we were right back where we started, the road we had turned off! We calmly rejoined the line of traffic and patiently we edged our way to the end of the road works. With now even more time lost, we were back, heading for Carlisle and the Scottish border.

Gretna was the first town in Scotland and as we passed through the town I recalled the last time I was there, I married Lucy. From here on we hugged the coast line until; as the day drew to an end we stopped off at Girvan, originally a fishing port on the west coast, now also a seaside resort. We found a campsite relatively easy where the lady in charge took a ten pound note from us as payment for our nights stay and then gave it back to us as a donation for our charity. We pitched our tent, had a shower and headed off into town.

The Famous Harbour Bar appeared to be the only pub around and inside it was something of a time warp, with a distinctive fisherman feel about the place. It had an assortment of bizarre pictures and objects on display around the room which was L shaped and had a corner bar, taking up almost half of the floor space. We sat away from the bar and enjoyed a simple but satisfying bar meal, accompanied by a pint of Guinness. The pub had a feel of how pubs used to be, full of locals and even a resident drunk, who in this case happened to be a woman. Although a little worse for wear, she probably wasn't actually the resident drunk, but she had no trouble in picking us out. After making enquiries as to why we were in Girvan, we had an interesting conversation with the lady, albeit slightly slurred from her side, about her mother and the difficulties she was having trying to control her diabetes. I offered some advice, which she seemed to take onboard and before leaving she reached into her purse and took out a crisp ten pound note for our charity. On leaving the premises ourselves, Ian pointed out an amusing sign on the bar that had caught his eye, it read.

AVOIDING THE WIFE
Bar phone tariff
£1 = "No, he's not here"
£2 = "You just missed him"
£3 = "he had one drink and left"
£4 = "he hasn't been in all day"
£5 = "never heard of him"

As we walked to the door something caught my eye and when I pointed it out to Ian, he pushed me from behind, out onto the street, saying.

"Paranoia!"

It was a photograph of a ventriloquist and his dummy.

Back at the tent we discussed our situation, we had made up some ground and it was now Friday 16th August and on the 17th we should have been at Jon o Groats. We decided, we could make up more time during the remaining week and we would continue our route as planned. Our next stop would be Fort William.

First we had to cross the Erskine Bridge near Glasgow, before we could head North West across the Highlands. The further north we rode the colder we became and then it started raining. After the torrential rain two days earlier our leather gloves never completely dried out, we stopped off in Paisley, at a motorcycle clothing shop and purchased some nylon waterproof gloves, along with neck scarves as the cold rain, could be like nails hitting you, especially with the open face helmets and our increased speed. So, gloved up and with scarves over our noses, we pushed on. The familiar combination of spectacular scenery and awful weather continued with us, we absorbed what we could but inevitably, much was missed.

'On the bonnie bonnie banks'

It seemed strange to be travelling with water to our right hand side, when we had set off with the sea on our left. The reason for this was, we were riding along the shores of Loch Lomond and here seemed a good spot to stop and take some snapshots.

'You take the high road'ZZ5

From here on, it was mountain roads which took us to great heights; it felt good to be able to relax without the worry of blowing a head gasket. We literally had our head in the clouds for a while, until inevitably we began our descent. With Britain's highest mountain, Ben Nevis in the foreground, we made our way down. Our only worry was the distance between petrol stations and I have to say, as we neared the bottom of the mountain the sight of a small fuel station was a welcome one. I pulled up at the pump and had to wait for the old lady to finish filling a car on the other side of the pump, none of this self serve nonsense in this neck of the woods I can tell you. After filling our tank and the spare Jerry can, the lady shouted the price to her husband who rang it into the till. Inside the shop was like a 1960's hardware store, selling everything from mousetraps to logs as well as pots and pans, it truly was like stepping back in time.

We continued along the desolate mountain roads until the weather took a turn for the worse. It had been damp and dismal all day, but then the heavens opened, it pissed it down! There was no more soaking up the scenery, it was just soaking up the rain. By the time we reached Fort William we were so wet we couldn't even contemplate camping. We went for the hotel option, finding a room at the Moorings Hotel. It may have been expensive but at least it was dry. We hung our clothes to dry in the room and had a shower, before enjoying a meal in the restaurant and then relaxing by the open fire. Yes, it was August and the fire was lit!

Sunday 18th, forecast for the day, rain! The previous evening had been a relaxing one, entertained by two young men, playing the accordion and the fiddle. Now it was back to reality, everything packed up and loaded onto the bike, topped up with oil and a good dosing of WD40 on the exposed electrics. A decision had been made to continue west until we reach the coast and then travel north.

It was Ian's turn on the bike so I took my position in the 'comfy sidecar.' Our hotel was situated on a tee junction, giving us three options. One was the road we had arrived on, the continuation of that would take us west to Mallaig and the other was clearly signposted to Inverness. We still hovered over a decision to take the road to Inverness and make up some time but we decided to stick to our guns.

As we set off Ian pulled up at the junction and asked if I was sure. I nodded and we headed west. Being in the sidecar did give some comfort, mainly keeping you dry from the waist down, but the full force of the weather was felt from the waist up. We battled against the rain for forty miles until we reached Mallaig, where the ferry across to the Isle of Skye was in dock. As the bike was performing well and the rain had eased we decided to make the most of the rest of our journey and take in places of interest, like the Isle of Skye. Ian pulled into the line of traffic, queuing for the ferry and as we drew closer we were stopped by a man in uniform.

"Ticket?"

"Yes, how much is it?"

Ian replied, the man shook his head saying.

"Do you no have a ticket?"

Ian removed his helmet and spoke slowly, thinking the man may be having difficulty understanding him.

"No, we want to buy one."

"Did you no book your'sel a ticket lad's? Well you cannay come on this ferry, were full!"

The uniformed man explained. We begged him to let us on but he refused and informed us that the next available ferry would be... Tomorrow!

With no other choice we turned around and headed north, but not for long, we were soon to learn that Mallaig was a dead end town, with only two ways out. One was by sea and the other was the road we had just travelled. After forty more miles we were back at Fort William, we stopped at the hotel to decide our next move and in no time, agreed to head straight for Inverness which meant leaving the coast, but would take us to the main route for Jon o Groats and once there we could resume our coastal route.

We turned left at the hotel and followed the signposts for Inverness. Our journey north, although inland was a pleasant one as we followed the shores of the infamous Loch Ness, unfortunately without any sign of a monster we rode on all the way to Inverness, we didn't stop but carried on to cross the Kessock Bridge and then the Moray Firth Bridge, we were now eating up the miles and before long crossed the Donorch Bridge. We had worked out that at this rate if we could reach the far north of Scotland and back to Inverness in the same day we would have made up all of the lost time, which meant we could really relax and enjoy the rest of the challenge.

I was now in the driving seat as we had swapped over in Inverness. The bike was running as sweet as a nut, apart from a slight vibration that had been with us since fitting this engine. The road was long and straight and I took advantage, maintaining a speed of around 60 mph and it felt good when suddenly BANG! followed by a loud clattering. I pulled in the clutch and coasted to the entrance of a field, where I turned off the main road. We both knew that following those kind of noises, good news does not appear.

While investigating the damage, we were joined by a passing motorist, Christian who offered to help but we were beyond help at this point. We had stripped the engine revealing that something serious had occurred, although we weren't sure exactly what. We had no choice but to call the AA.

It wasn't too long before the recovery truck arrived; I only had limited cover with the AA, enough for them to send a truck from the nearest garage, who would take us back to their premises. Bannerman Garage of Tain, turned up and winched the outfit onto the back of the truck. The driver took us to Tain, a town famous for the malt whiskey distillery, Glenmorangie, approximately five miles from where we broke down. The bike and sidecar was unloaded and placed inside the garage at Bannerman's, we took off the panniers and the driver closed and locked the doors. It was Sunday afternoon and we needed somewhere to stay. The driver took us to a hotel in the town and told us to return to the garage in the morning.

The hotel had no vacancies and neither did the next one we tried, it seemed like the whole town was booked up. The reason for this was, apparently an oil company had reopened one of their terminals close to the town, finding work for lots of people, not all of them local. The last hotel we tried didn't have a room but the girl on reception was very helpful and recommended a B&B, she telephoned them and reserved us the one remaining room. It was a short walk from where we were, although when carrying panniers, even a short walk can be taxing.

A view from the cab of Bannerman's truck

The place was ok but terribly expensive, probably why they had a room spare. When we were told that breakfast was served from 8.30am we asked if we could have ours served earlier as we needed to be at the garage for 7am. The answer was simply no! We settled in to our room and began the difficult task of removing the blackened oil from our hands, before taking a shower. We ate in one of the hotels in the town, where we discussed our situation and decided, no matter how bad it was, we would find a way to fix it. What we needed now was liquid refreshment to assist in the numbing of our pain.

Tain is a small town, not much more than a village, where we managed to find the Star Inn, a small pub just off the Main street, it was a stone fronted building and were it not for the sign hanging on the wall outside, could easily have been mistaken for a house with just a narrow pavement between it and the road. Inside we ordered a couple of drinks and sat by the front window to enjoy. We enjoyed a couple more and as the evening went on the ridiculous situations that had brought us there, somehow seemed less ridiculous. During a visit to the bar I was joined by a gentleman introducing himself as Chris, he insisted on paying for our drinks as I placed the order. Who was I to argue? He added a pint of Guinness for himself to the order and Ian joined us at the bar.

Chris, a man who I would guess was in his forties, seemed glad of someone to talk to. I think he picked us out because like him, we didn't have a Scottish accent. During our conversation we were joined by another, a rather drunken specimen who definitely spoke with a Scottish accent, so strong in fact, combined with the slur of his speech, it was almost impossible to decipher. It wasn't difficult to work out, from the aggression in his voice and his mannerisms, he was picking for a fight, Chris stepped back while Ian and I watched in amazement at how this man was managing to stay upright. I often wonder why some men become violent after consuming alcohol, just at the point when they can barely even raise a fist. The man was suddenly removed when an apologetic local man grabbed the back of his shirt and pulled him away. We resumed our conversation.

Chris told us how he was working in Tain, for the oil company as a chemical engineer and staying in a rented house just down the road, we told him of our disastrous journey and our attempt at raising money for our charity, Chris admiring our efforts, made a donation of a tenner, all in all we had an enjoyable evening in the Star Inn, a good few drinks, met a half decent bloke, enjoyed good conversation and even experienced some drunken aggression. It reminded me of home.

As we were about to leave we mentioned our need for a café breakfast early in the morning, to which Chris replied.

"There are no café's open that early around here, they only cater for the tourists."

I thought for a moment and then said.

"We'll have to go back to the B&B for breakfast; after all we've paid for it."

Ian shook his head saying.

"No, it's too far, we'll wait until the café opens and have a late breakfast."

Just then Chris interrupted.

"No need, come and have breakfast with me, my house is close to the garage and I'm up early every morning."

We didn't have to consider the offer for too long, I gave him a quick reply.

"Ok, what's your address?"

Chris gave a detailed description of the location, Ian reiterated.

"So, past the hotel, second left, third house on the right, red door?"

"Yes that's it, come straight in the door will be open. Don't worry if you hear voices, that'll be Archie."

"Archie?"

Ian asked rather puzzled, as Chris had mentioned he was staying on his own.

"Yes I'm a bit of a children's entertainer in my spare time, Archie is my vent dummy."

At this point I was glad I had consumed a reasonable amount of alcohol, because to say the least, I was shocked! Things remained silent for a while before Ian broke the ice.

"Is it a modern puppet?"

Chris replied in a jolly sort of way.

"Oh no, he's older than me."

I felt an immediate need to leave this situation as I was beginning to question things in my head.

"We'll see you about seven then." Ian said, shaking Chris's hand.

We took a long stroll back to the guest house and agreed; weird it may be but not beyond the bounds of possibility and things would seem different in the morning.

In the morning, things were pretty much the same, we had to face whatever we may find wrong with the bike and we had memories of the previous night, where we had met a stranger in a pub, who had offered us breakfast at his home, with a warning that we may encounter voices as we entered the house, voices of a conversation between the stranger and his companion Archie! However, at 6.30 we left the digs with our luggage, as we had no intention of returning and we walked toward the town. As usual, it was further than we remembered and the weight of the panniers soon took its toll. We passed the closed café as well as the street where the pub was and my belly was rumbling. We turned a corner and the hotel where we had eaten the night before came into view. Decision time, as this was the same hotel used in the directions to Chris and Archie's house.

A decision was made based on hunger; we passed the hotel and looked for the second left turn. It was only a short distance before we turned onto the road, which was a slight incline; we walked up the hill toward a row of terraced houses on the right hand side.

"One, two, three... That's not fuckin' red!

Ian said loudly and disappointed. The door we faced was not red, it was white and looking around there was no red door on any of the houses.

"Maybe it's the wrong road."

I suggested.

"Well there's only one other road and that's the one we just passed."

Ian pointed out and it was a valid point, there were only two roads off to the left of the bottom road. We took a look and there were no red doors, we tried the only road to the right and there were no red doors. We stopped and looked at the facts. Either, the man had forgotten where he lived, or he had painted his door a different colour and forgotten about it, or he was lying. The only other options begin to get a little, 'out of this world' so we won't be going there. We headed for the garage instead, which wasn't too far away.

Chapter eight

Arrival at the garage was a welcoming one; it was a large concern with lots of recovery trucks and lots of garage space. The staff were helpful and the owner, more than we could have asked for. To give you an idea of the size of this place, the main building could accommodate several HGV vehicles complete with trailers along with half a dozen cars or more. At one end there was an office and a locker room with wash room and toilet. Our bike was parked just inside the doorway behind a hydraulic vehicle lift, which was supporting a Jeep at the time, in for repair. Andy the boss, agreed to let us use his garage to strip the engine. We made a start but overtook by hunger; we decided to hunt for food. Asking the lads in the garage where we might eat didn't help much, until one of them said he thought there was a café in a supermarket not too far away. He gave us directions, which we followed.

"Out of the gates, turn right, first left then follow the road to the end, the supermarket is there on the left hand side."

The left turn took us onto an industrial estate where the road was long and curved. We walked and we talked and we walked and the talking lessened, as our mouths were dry from the thirst created by the previous night's indulgence, so we walked and we walked…

It was a warm summer morning in the Highlands and with our tongues almost touching the floor, we eventually saw a building in the distance, resembling a supermarket. It had a haze of heat lifting from its flat roof and disappearing into the sun. It was another oasis in our desert. Ian increased his pace and the distance between us lengthened, he could see the finish line and had begun his final sprint to the post. Not far behind him, I arrived at the Co-op to find it almost empty. We must have been the first customers, as the place appeared deserted, we asked a staff member about the location of a café and she pointed to the far corner of the building. Sure enough, there was an area seemingly designated for the consumption of food, the only person we could see was a lady wiping tables. Ian asked her.

"Can we order some food luv?"

The lady replied with a disappointing look on her face and shaking her head.

"We don't open 'till ten, you can maybe pick up a wee sandwich in the shop."

I looked at my phone, it was 8.30. We found the refrigerators in the main store, picked ourselves a sandwich and a drink each and paid at the tills.

During our walk back along the long curved road, we consumed our pre packed, chilled egg and bacon roll, delicious! We arrived back at the garage feeling slightly better than when we had left.

It didn't take too long to remove the engine as we had removed a lot of the parts by the roadside. We carried the engine to the bench in order to split the crankcase and before long we had our answer. The crankshaft had snapped in two. Yes, it had broken in half!

We now had to locate a new crankshaft, which was not so easy as it had been upgraded to a needle roller big end bearing, and there was the answer. The upgrade had been done by Henry. I gave him a call, he was shocked at the amount of misfortune we had encountered and even more so at the crank breaking. He knew the engine and remembered rebuilding it, it had done around five thousand miles since the rebuild and he could offer no explanation as to why it should break. He did have another, brand new crankshaft and agreed to send it to us by courier. I gave him the address and he took my telephone number to text me the tracking number, job done!

Broke down again!

Where's the engine?

Here it is!

We now had to find ourselves a campsite and after a little enquiring, we learned that there was one, close to the Dornoch Bridge, not far from where we had originally broke down. We ordered a taxi, which arrived shortly after we had tidied up and moved the bike to the back of the garage, out of the way. We packed up most of the spares in boxes provided by Andy and we stored them in the locker room. The luggage and camping equipment was put in the taxi, along with ourselves and we left to go camping.

Our luxury accommodation

At the Dornoch Caravan and Camping site we were directed to a plot where we pitched our tent. The campsite was isolated, squeezed tightly between a road and a railway line. There was a pub which turned out to be a converted railway station, there was a Jehovah's Witness Hall and that was it! There didn't appear to be a shop of any kind, you can usually buy essential things from reception, but not here.

The surrounding landscape was pretty flat and we were on the coast of the Dornoch Firth, an estuary on the east coast of the Scottish Highlands. When travelling in the taxi it seemed only a few minutes before we arrived at the campsite, so it could only be a few miles away from Tain. We decided to go back into town to pick up a few things, at least something for breakfast.

While discussing which mode of transport we might use for our return to town, we were standing close to reception, near the entrance to the site, when we were approached by a young woman. She introduced herself as Alice and asked if we would like a lift into town. We accepted the offer and she told us.

"He'll be here in a minute."

True enough, a car pulled into the site and stopped by our side, we got in the back of the car while Alice got in the front.

"This is Stevie."

She said as she put on her seat belt.

"I've told them you'd give 'em a lift into town Stevie is that alright?"

Stevie didn't answer but Alice carried on.

"Aye, it's fine, Stevie's great, he doesn't mind."

During the short journey I got the impression that Stevie and Alice had a one sided relationship. He was older than her and for no particular reason Alice mentioned that they were 'just good friends' a phrase often used when at least one of them would like to be more than 'just good friends' in this case Stevie. I know this is a deep analysis of two people I only met for a few moments, but sometimes you just know. Of course, I'm probably barking completely up the wrong tree!

Stevie dropped us in town, where we got out of the car along with Alice, who said goodbye and walked off, we walked in the same direction but she soon disappeared into the bustling crowd.

We found a shop and picked up a few bits, mainly milk and pots of porridge that can be made by simply adding hot water. We had a brief wander around but decided to make our way back to the campsite, this time we decided to walk.

The main A9 was further away from the town than we had anticipated and as we walked in the direction of it, I recognised a certain flat roofed building to our right. It was the Co-op, the one we seemed to have walked miles to get to, yet it was literally about half the distance from the garage, if you walked the other way. Oh well, you live and learn. Eventually we reached the main road and it was simply a matter of turning right and following your nose. There were no footpaths on the road, so we used the grass verge, when there was a grass verge, when that disappeared we were walking on the road, which can be a hair raising experience at times with the traffic whizzing past, almost touching you. There came a break when we reached the distillery, which had a small road running in front of it parallel with the main road. Although tempted by thoughts of a wee dram of single malt, we resisted temptation and pushed on. The small road soon came to an end and we rejoined the main road by climbing over a small stone wall. You could now see the bridge in the distance, which was where we needed to be and the only thing between it and us was a long road and a lot of cows. The road was now running by the side of fields full of cattle, some cows with calves and some just bullocks that would crowd toward us as we passed. The lack of pavement caused us to swap sides and walk on the left of the road where there was now a grass verge. Eventually and much later than we envisaged, we arrived back at the campsite.

After a shower and shave we had to come to a decision, where would we spend our evening? Faced with so many options, we narrowed it down to two and although a difficult choice, we decided to give the Kingdom Hall of Jehovah's Witnesses a miss, therefore settling on the pub, a wise choice I thought.

The Dornoch Bridge Inn, was a pleasant place to eat, good food and a cosy room with a log fire burning, made you feel at ease. We couldn't even discuss our plans for the next day, at least not involving the bike. We did look back at the previous evening's experience and agreed it was weird when I suddenly remembered something.

"At least we got a tenner out of him for the char…"

I had put my fingers into the small pocket of my jeans, the one inside the right hand front pocket, to feel for the ten pound note.

"It's gone, it's not here!"

I checked the rest of my pockets but I knew where I had put it, I always put charity money in that pocket so it doesn't get mixed up with my own.

"Did you take it out when we got to the digs?"

Ian asked, trying to help.

"No, I definitely put it in here and now it's gone!"

I thought for a moment, took a sip of Guinness and said.

"Don't you think this is all getting a bit too strange?"

"What do ya mean?"

Ian asked, I thought about what I had just said and gave a quick reply.

"Nothing, I'm talking bollocks, I must have took it out."

We finished the evening off by the log fire, enjoying a different, more relaxed conversation before returning to our ¾ size tent for a night's sleep.

The next day we took a taxi back to the garage after our suitable breakfast of porridge and tea, prepared by myself. It was now Tuesday 20th August; we should have been in Aberdeen after covering the whole of the west and northern coast of Scotland. We hadn't even reached the north coast, even after cutting out a large piece of the west coast. Our hopes were now pinned on the arrival of the crankshaft, which had a long way to travel.

The only way to find out what was happening was to go online with the smart phone and use the tracking number henry had sent me. This may sound like an easy thing to do, but believe me, it was proving to be difficult as both of our phones had flat batteries, I needed to use a mains charger and the only plug socket I could find spare was in the garage on a pillar in the darkest part of the building. The socket was high up and the cable short, I had to hold up the phone and put in a number containing more digits than Tommy Lipton's got tea leaves, none of this helped by the fact that I didn't have my reading glasses with me and as anyone over the age of forty will tell you, makes it damn near impossible! Eventually, I receive information that the parcel has made it to a depot in Coventry, which meant it still had a long way to travel.

We spent some time doing other bits on the bike but without the spares we were at a loss. We took ourselves into town where, Ian had a haircut and bought some reading glasses, we had lunch in the 'tourist' café, nice but expensive. Before long we were out of things to do, we had seen a sign for a golf course, but Ian had been suffering with back pain, as I nearly always am. And swinging a golf club is not the best therapy. We decided to go back to the campsite but while wandering we had drifted away from the town centre and toward the beach.

Amazingly we seemed to have forgotten how taxing the walk back had been just the day before, and we decided to walk along the beach, at least some of the way. The beach turned out to be pebbles, large and small, squillions of them and not a hint of sand. We hoped that before long we would come across a pathway leading back to the road, so we plodded on regardless. Walking on pebbles in canvas pumps soon gets to be a painful experience, but not soon enough to have stopped us travelling too far to now contemplate turning back. With no sign of a path, we realised that somehow there was a railway line between us and the road, now we needed a foot bridge and there was no sign of one of them either. The railway line ran along the coast, almost on the beach in places, we were trapped.

Apart from the endless amount of pebbles, we came across pieces of old cars, including an engine, gearbox and axles. We started to identify the different parts through our knowledge of scrap cars; the engine was a BMC A series from something like a Morris Minor. All of the different parts were rusted to extreme from the salt water with the rust disguising the parts, it kept us occupied as we trudged along the beach. We soon came level with the distillery, still separated by the railway which started to drift away from the beach and eventually we had fields between it and us. We were still confined to the beach however but now it was the cows!

As I have mentioned, my brother, Ian is a larger build than I am and he likes to think he's a bit of a tough nut who fears no one and no thing. But for the second time on this journey I discovered a definite fear. The first was the fear of confined spaces and the second was the fear of cows! He absolutely refused to cross the field full of cows and so we continued our painful walk along the pebble beach, all the way to the start of the Dornoch Bridge, where we climbed the embankment and walked along the road, crossing the railway and to our destination.

Back at the tent we rested our sore feet; Ian took to the tent while I stitched some rips in our biker jackets, using a handy repair kit supplied by some hotel or other. Eventually, I had to join Ian in the tent as I became under attack by a swarm of biting midges.

That evening we visited the pub for a meal and while there we met a young couple who chatted with us and after they left a message on the charity website.

"Bumped into the lad's while staying at the Dornoch campsite and the wine was flowing! Hope the bike was fixed in Tain and the rest of your journey was successful! All the best. Ben."

How nice.

In the morning we packed our tent and panniers; and after our porridge and tea breakfast we carried them to reception where we ordered a taxi to take us back to the garage. We also paid our campsite fee, without discount but with some heated discussion, involving at times, some angry swearing! Some of these Scotsmen can be very touchy about money.

It was lunch time before the parts arrived, we hastily unpacked, eager to confirm we had what we needed. We did, now all we had to do was put the mass of engine parts back together in the correct order. We set about the task, encouraged by some of the mechanics working in the garage that day, who would give remarks as they passed by.

"Rather you than me lads!"

"Are you sure you're gonnie know how to do that?"

"I wouldney know where to start wi that lot!"

Despite such professional advice, we soldiered on and before long we had something in front of us that resembled a motorcycle engine. It took us the rest of the afternoon to finish the rebuild and refit the engine into the bike, and we were still working on it when it came time for the garage to close. Andy came up with a solution. He closed the front gates and gave us his telephone number, allowing us to stay and finish the job. All we had to do then was give him a call when we'd finished and he would come and lock up.

A sandwich and crisps from the petrol station for our evening meal and we eventually had the bike running again. We cleaned up after ourselves and called Andy, while waiting for his return we packed our luggage on the outfit and took it outside ready to leave. Andy arrived and we attempted to thank him suitably for all his help while he locked up, but reality was, our gratitude was impossible to put into words. He was a very helpful, trusting and generous man to whom we will be eternally grateful.

It was now early Wednesday evening, we made a decision. We would travel north to Jon o Groats; spend the night there, then go 'Hell for leather' back down to Inverness and from there across the north coast of Scotland. That was our plan.

We set off with Ian on the bike and me in the chair, going seemed good apart from the throttle cable having a tendency to stick. We crossed the Dornoch Bridge and passed the place of our original breakdown when we heard a loud knocking sound. Ian pulled in the clutch but the sound continued and as we slowed the knocks lessened. This suggests that it was from the transmission, a right turn became visible in the fading light, Ian turned off the main road and brought the bike to a halt.

A quick inspection revealed nothing, a sign post told us the town of Dornoch was only a couple of miles away. We travelled the two miles tenderly, accompanied by the knocking sound until we arrived in the small town. It was a quiet evening as we pulled into a pub car park. We had to search for a container to catch the oil we were about to drain, Ian found a plastic container in the bins which we cut the side off to collect the oil. We then took off the primary cover and removed the alternator and clutch. Everything seemed fine, we rebuilt it and was about to go to the other side of the bike and take apart the gearbox when Ian stopped me.

"I don't believe it! Look at this."

He shouted in an exited outburst. His head was down and he pointed toward the rear wheel, using his phone as a torch.

"It's a broken spoke!"

Ian exclaimed. I took a closer look and sure enough, one of the spokes had broken and was protruding outward, causing it to hit the frame at least twice for every revolution of the wheel.

We took a moment to consider the reality... Things were not too bad; they had been scary, but not too bad. I tucked the broken spoke behind one of its neighbours, then we put the bits back on the bike, packed away the tools and off we went again. We didn't get far! Just a few yards and the throttle cable snapped. We fitted a new one under the light of a street lamp, outside someone's house in an almost deserted town.

Eventually, we were ready to leave once more, As soon as we left the town, we were surrounded by a dense fog and light rain. Hardly able to see our hands in front of us, we struggled on until the head light beam started to grow duller and the ammeter showed a discharge. The bike had stopped charging and the battery was almost flat. Switching off the headlamp gave us some grace and I had fitted an auxiliary battery which I switched on but inevitably that began to fade and we were forced to stop. A sign for the Highlands Inn, drew us close, in fact into the car park, but there was no room at the inn.

It was now quite late and the young man behind the bar agreed to let us sleep on the floor in one of the downstairs rooms, the one with a pool table. He even served us a much needed pint before leaving us to it and locking us in the place.

We paid for a breakfast the following morning, before checking over the bike. The alternator was only charging intermittently and then only a trickle of power. It did however allow us to continue our journey, at least while it was light and we refrained from using anything that may drain the batteries, like indicators and especially phone chargers.

Now devastated by the recent series of events and disasters, we were so far behind our only option was to take a direct route to Edinburgh. Ian took to the saddle and rode relentlessly across Scotland. Before reaching Edinburgh we made an essential stop at Mc D's for lunch, which left us in trouble as the batteries were flat and the bike refused to start. Luckily we spotted a man in a van eating his lunch. We got him to hook up to us using a couple of lengths of earth cable as makeshift jump leads and after half hour with his van running we were able to carry on.

Another stop was soon needed as we had been losing oil, a similar problem to the one we had with the previous engine. We stopped at a car spares to buy oil and while there we purchased a lead with cigar socket ends that we could use to plug into the socket in our sidecar and to any willing vehicle to obtain a charge. Having topped up with oil, we left the oil filler cap off, as before and carried on as best we could.

Crossing the Fourth Road Bridge felt like an achievement, leading us passed Edinburgh and on to the inevitable return to England. During urban driving we tended to use the brakes more often, draining power through the brake lights. The bike had stopped charging altogether now and we were forced to pull over into a lay-by.

Rescued yet again! By a complete stranger who pulled up and offered his help, we plugged in the lead from our vehicle to his and received some volts, afterwards the helpful man gave us a tow to start the bike as the compression was getting low, making it difficult to start. We think it may have been due to the bike overheating for some reason. I took my turn on the bike and while riding around a roundabout at Berwick upon Tweed, just inside the English border the engine stopped. We pushed the outfit to a safer place, a small triangular paved area by the side of a house, close to the roundabout, just big enough for us to squeeze both us and the combination on.

Things were now looking grim. Stuck on a main road with nowhere for anyone to pull up and help, I knocked on the house door but no one was home. We were Knackered!

Neither of us could work out how we had managed to get this far, nor had we any idea how we could get any further. We decided to attend to a small problem we had been having with the throttle cable, since fitting it the engine idling speed was too fast and we needed to shorten the outer cable. We stripped the twist grip and out of nowhere a man appeared, he asked.

"Do you need any help?"

He was an older gentleman and he began to reminisce.

"I've been in your shoes a time or two, I used to have a BSA an' it was always breaking down, I remember one time…"

Ian interrupted the man.

"We could do with a vehicle to give us some charge,"

"I'll get the car then."

The man said before disappearing from whence he came. It turned out he had seen us in distress as he travelled the roundabout and drove back on himself, parked the car and walked to us.

He pulled his car alongside us and put the hazards on. We plugged in the lead and continued with the throttle cable. The man got involved and with three pairs of hands we finally managed it. Before leaving, the kind gentleman left us with a gift of a multi tool penknife. We thanked him and continued on.

After around three hundred mile that day we finally stopped at a hotel just outside Newcastle. The bike was running like a sick pig, we had retightened the cylinder head three times since the rebuild, our legs were covered in oil and we were ready for a shower. Ian kept the engine running while I enquired inside. A room was available and I signalled from the doorway for Ian to cut the engine.

The Waterford Lodge Hotel, Morpeth. A few miles north of Newcastle. Morpeth is a historic town of Northumberland and very picturesque. It was late and we were both in need of a severe degreasing. We checked in to the hotel and took our luggage to the room, where we did the best we could to clean ourselves up. Having been told that food would be served in the bar until nine oclock, we made sure we were down there by eight forty-five. Not for the first time on this trip we were informed that the kitchens were closed. Too exhausted to argue, we settled for a pint and a bag of crisps.

We had travelled three hundred miles with the bike not charging, we had used almost as much oil as we had petrol, but we were here!

Ian received a call from Vicky asking him where we were, she also informed him that we had to be in Scarborough the following day as a welcoming party had been arranged and the local press would be there. I heard Ian saying.

"We will be there, I promise, yes we will be there!"

I always hated it when we had a time to be somewhere, because so far we hadn't made any of them.

I told Ian, "We'd better be up early in the morning, we'll have to take off the cylinder head again; I think it may be the gasket."

Ian agreed.

In the morning we were up early, enjoying breakfast in the dining room, we then packed everything away before pushing the bike into the car park at the rear of the hotel where we could take it to pieces, again! As we were in need of more oil, I left Ian working on the bike and I walked into town to find a car spares shop.

I enjoyed the walk through the town centre, it was a warm sunny morning and the thought of arriving in Scarborough later that day put a spring in my step. I located a spares shop where I bought oil and I picked up a cycle inner tube while I was there. On the way back, I stopped at a charity shop to ask for some old clothes we could use as rags to soak up the oil. The assistants were very obliging and gave me two double bed sheets and to thank them, I made a donation to the charity.

Back at the hotel, Ian had the bike in bits. I ripped up one of the sheets into hand wipe sized pieces and joined in the work. After refitting the cylinder head and all the other parts, we topped up with oil and I took the new inner tube and cut through it making a long rubber tube. I connected one end over the oil filler neck and threaded the length over the frame and left it trailing by the rear wheel. We collared one of the car park users to hook up and give us some charge, and we were ready to go, again.

The aim now was to get to Scarborough no matter what. Lucy had booked into a hotel there and Vicky was staying with some friends, the ones organizing the welcome party. We set off, taking the main A1 south to clock up some miles. The inner tube was working, taking the excess compression and spilled oil away from my leg and we were making progress. We had crossed the Blaydon Bridge, passing Newcastle and going good, as we approached the Durham exit, the engine died! I pulled in the clutch and free wheeled onto the slip road where we ground to a halt.

I was now losing the will to live and Ian didn't appear much happier. There was still power in the batteries, but no compression at all, as I discovered when trying to kick start the bike. I had my suspicions of what the problem may be, I removed the spark plug as we were joined by a bloke on a trials bike. He offered to help, but at this stage there was nothing he could do. I took a thin straight stick from the bushes and placed it down the plug hole. I turned over the engine with the kick start lever and brought the piston to the top, then moving the stick over the top of the piston, it suddenly dropped down. This confirmed my suspicions; there was a hole in the top of the piston.

The reason for me suspecting this was because the engine appeared to have been running too hot, it had been pinking as I rode the dual carriageway, probably pulling air from somewhere, weakening the fuel mixture. I had kept going in hope of reaching the Durham turn off, where we were going to take the more scenic coastal route.

We had reached the exit but not as we had planned. With the help of the trials biker, we pushed the outfit along the slip road, onto the roundabout where we turned left, downhill toward a park & ride car park. We entered through the exit route but by now we didn't care. Ian jumped on the bike as it coasted into the car parking area where he parked up. It was now about two o'clock in the afternoon.

All hopes of finishing our journey had now ended and we simply wanted to get to Scarborough to be with our wives. We asked a bus driver how we could achieve this and if it could be done by four o'clock. He shook his head and suggested we took a train from Durham. The security staff at the park & ride agreed to us leaving the bike there and even said they would put a camera on it. We had a wash in the toilets, took off the panniers and leaving everything else with the bike, we took a lift on one of the buses into town, the driver dropped us as close as he could to the railway station and wished us well.

A pair of one way tickets to Scarborough gave us time on the train to realise our dream was over. We had done what we said we would never do, we had given up. The bike had beaten us. The dummy had won; we had been run into the ground and could fight no more.

Chapter nine

Of course we hadn't given up, not entirely. It was Friday afternoon before a bank holiday weekend when disaster struck. Even if we had found a piston, getting it sent to us before the following Tuesday would have been close to impossible. Ian had stated from the beginning that he could not go over the three weeks we had allowed because of work commitments.

The following day I picked up my van and trailer from Ian's house and drove back to Durham to collect the bike. The security staff gave me a push onto the trailer and said that it had been the star attraction in the car park, gathering crowds of camera clicking admirers each time a bus unloaded.

We had decided that I would take the bike home, repair it and return to Durham to complete journey at the first convenient time.

Removing the cylinder head revealed what I had expected. There was a hole burned in the top of the piston. I telephoned Henry, who agreed to send me a new piston, I told him not to rush and to include a new alternator.

With the engine rebuilt, I somehow didn't feel confident about setting off for the final leg. I decided to have a test run, for which I would need a passenger. Unfortunately, no one was available, or should I say willing to join me, so I filled the sidecar with bricks, roughly to the equivalent weight of Ian, a lot of bricks! And just so I didn't feel alone, I sat Charlie on the pile of bricks.

Close to where I live, there are two roads which cross the Pennines, one is the Snake Pass, the other is the Woodhead Pass. I decided I would travel over the hills via the Woodhead and return via the Snake. These roads are notoriously treacherous during the winter, but can be pleasantly exhilarating during the summer, although many motorcyclists have lost their lives on some of the sunniest days over these hills.

I set off for my test run without notifying anyone, it was just me and the moth eaten dummy. I figured if anything was going to happen, it would happen now, if I were to admit belief in the unbelievable, then it had every chance of showing its face now and coming right out in the open.

I cannot deny my heart was in my mouth for the first few miles; after all I didn't have my brother sat beside me in case it all went tits up! I was on my own, apart from Charlie, yet after a while, in the sunshine and feeling the steady beat of the engine beneath me, I began to enjoy the ride, in fact it turned out to be a very pleasant journey, I ran into some fog on the snake but I returned home without experiencing a single misfire. The bike was running like a clock.

At home I returned Charlie to his hook on the wall of the garage; it almost seemed as if he was grinning as I stepped back from him. I removed the bricks from the sidecar and telephoned Ian to let him know the bike was fixed.

It was a Saturday and I had acquired a helper. Chris, the guy who followed us at the beginning of our trip had agreed to join us when we took the outfit on the trailer back to Durham. He would then follow us back in case anything should go wrong. We picked Ian up on the way and returned to Durham, close to the spot where we abandoned the bike. We unloaded the bike in the rain, Ian started it, I jumped in the sidecar and after only a few yards the engine started to misfire. Immediate thoughts were of damp getting on the ignition lead. WD40 sprayed on everything didn't cure it, eventually we discovered a piece of gasket missing on the inlet manifold, it wouldn't have caused the misfire but it could explain the overheating, making the engine run very weak or lean.

Having replaced the gasket we set off again but before long the misfire returned. We stopped in a lay by and changed the condenser. Hey Presto! That was it.

It was now pissing it down with rain, we set off again and this time we were flying. Going like the clappers on a duel carriage way when. BANG! Clatter, clonk bang! Clonk, clatter bang! Ian coasted into a pub car park. The engine sounded like it had fallen to pieces.

Soaking wet, moral lower than the tarmac we stood on; we loaded up the bike onto the trailer and headed home. We stopped off for lunch where Ian made his feelings very clear. We had done all that we could and we could do no more. I suggested that as we had to cross the Humber Bridge to get to Ian's house, we should take some photos as we crossed, even showing the bike on the trailer, so we could perhaps post them on Facebook and our website, to give some sort of conclusion. It was agreed.

I drove the van back, feeling pretty shit about everything, when we arrived at the bridge. I pulled up at the kiosk to pay the toll, where I was given the final kick in the balls! Apparently the bridge was closed to vehicles towing trailers because of high winds.

It now seemed to me that the Classic Coastal Sidecar Challenge 2013 was destined to fail. No matter what we did or how determined we were, something stopped us, it was as if we had been cursed! Right from the moment we decided to do it, or could it have been, from the moment we acquired the sidecar and its contents?

Back home I couldn't even bring myself to unload the outfit off the trailer for a couple of days. Eventually, I did and I stripped the engine to discover the con-rod had broken, snapped off just below the piston. This sort of thing does not happen! Not to normal people anyway.

After it snapped, the con-rod had gone on to beat itself against the piston and barrel, damaging them beyond repair. So another call to Henry was required and he sent me the parts as he usually did. I had to strip the engine to the bare bones again, splitting the crankcase and the crankshaft. At least there was no rush anymore, and I patiently rebuilt and refitted the engine, with Charlie watching over me. At one point I have to admit I told him in no uncertain terms.

"YOU'RE NOT GOING TO BEAT ME YOU LITTLE BASTARD!"

With the bike running again, I toyed with the idea of sneaking off to the Humber Bridge and riding across, just to satisfy my own mind, I took the outfit for a run to where Lucy works a few miles away and on the return journey, as I approached a roundabout for the M1, I thought, sod it I'm gonna do this and as I made this consideration, I noticed the ammeter on the bike went to discharge. Another coincidence! My mind was changed, I took the bike home and as I pulled onto the drive it began to charge again!

As we moved into September, I couldn't get it out of my mind. After some logical thinking, my old self returned and I now had to cross the bridge with that motorcycle and definitely that sidecar, no matter what!

I had a plan, to put the outfit on the trailer, then taking Lucy with me; we drive to the Humber Bridge. We park up, I take the bike off the trailer and ride it across the bridge, while Lucy remains on the south side and on the return crossing she takes the appropriate photos, so we would have the evidence and the closure. Surprisingly, Lucy agreed.

I loaded the outfit onto the trailer after checking every moving part on the machine was working correctly, then while strapping it to the trailer; I considered how the photos would look with no passenger in the sidecar. I had an idea. It was one of those light bulb on the head moments. I had the perfect passenger. I informed Lucy, we were ready to go and she followed me out of the house, our driveway is to the rear of the house and as we walked passed the garage Lucy shrieked, before shouting at me.

"Take that thing out of there or I will not be coming with you!"

I explained things to her.

"We need someone in the sidecar; if he doesn't go then you'll have to, just for the photos."

Confused and in fear of being compared to 'Olive' from 'On the Buses' she got in the van.

We had only travelled a couple of miles when suddenly, all of the instruments on the van stopped working, including the speedo and the fuel gauge. I turned off the main road, onto a side road where I stopped the van. I did all the usual stuff, like checking fuses and connections, everything seemed fine. I checked the lights and found that the only thing working was the indicators.

This was bizarre, almost everything electrical on the van had packed in, yet the engine still ran, all of the fuses were ok and I was beginning to think I was losing my mind! I sat back in the seat and Lucy put her hand on my leg, she spoke softly.

"Let's go back, we'll have to do it another day."

The thought of yet another obstacle began to make my blood boil! I started the van, spun it around in the road and carried on toward the motorway.

"What are you doing, where are you going?

She asked in a confused panic.

"If we get back before dark then I won't need the lights, I'll try not to use the brakes and I can guess the speed. I'm going and I will not be stopped!"

I replied in a sort of, loud tone.

It seemed better to avoid further conversation as we joined the M1, and then almost immediately the M18 taking us gradually away from the main motorway. Never before had I been more determined to complete a job than on this day. A few miles went by and we passed the A1 turn off, the road ahead was long and straight. I was keeping up with the rest of the traffic when I felt a bump, as if we'd run over something. Lucy looked around, confused.

"What was that?"

She asked. Answering honestly I said.

"I don't know."

Then I looked in the mirror…

I can honestly say that I have never before, or since been so shocked by an image reflected in a door mirror. There was a vehicle following behind, I pulled into the hard shoulder to get a better view, and there it was. A motorcycle and sidecar in the nearside lane of the M18 motorway, travelling at around 50mph with no rider, just a ventriloquists dummy sat in the sidecar, travelling open mouthed into the oncoming draught.

To say this moment was surreal would be an understatement. I could hear no sound, I couldn't speak. I had to wind down the window and put my head out to see if it was really there… It was. I slowed down, allowing the bike to draw by my side; slowly the sidecar came into view through my side window, until the dummy was almost sat beside me. Suddenly his head turned toward me, I gasped for breath as his jaw began chattering open and shut as if he was laughing at me. I felt as if I was in one of the many weird dreams I have, but this was no dream. This was a living nightmare, and I was living it!

I was brought back to earth when Lucy shouted.

"Stop the van!"

I suddenly realised what I had to do. I edged the van closer to the sidecar until the wheel of the van connected with the wheel of the sidecar, puncturing the sidecar wheel and causing it to slow down, I grabbed hold of it with my arm out of the window and held it steady, making sure it didn't drift into the outside lane, where traffic flowed by with people staring in disbelief.

I slowed down, allowing the bike to slow with me, I let go and pulled ahead, stopping the van and quickly and running out into the carriageway. I jumped onto the still moving bike and steered it into the hard shoulder, bringing it to a standstill behind the trailer.

I grabbed hold of that fucking dummy and ripped it out of its seat, I threw it to the floor and grabbing hold of its hair I pulled the grotesque ugly little head from its body. Lucy was out of the van now and screamed at me to stop the assault on the dummy. I threw it into the van and took out two hi-vis vests and a pair of ramps, instructing Lucy to put on one of the vests; I did the same and went on to place the ramps onto the back of the trailer.

"Give us a push."

I shouted as I took hold of the handle bars, we quickly pushed the outfit onto the trailer. The securing straps had been ripped to pieces, I had it improvise by using a thin luggage strap to tie the front wheel to the frame that it sits in, I did the best I could to fasten the back down with a ripped strap and beckoned Lucy to get in the van. We set off slowly, rejoining the main carriageway.

The next turnoff came pretty quickly and I gladly took the exit, turning left at the first junction, I pulled up on a quiet road leading to an industrial estate. I switched off the engine, took in a deep breath and began to realise the possible consequences of what had just happened.

Lucy looked at me and said.

"That really frightened you, didn't it?"

I gave her my reply.

"That scared the living shit out of me!"

I went on to point out.

"We were so close to a multi-car pile up!"

The reality was terrifying; we really had been so close to a possible disaster. I took myself out of the van and made the outfit more secure by using a piece of rope I had in the van and we took ourselves home.

I have suffered from severe shock three times in my life, the first while working at the scrap yard. I was melting aluminium gearboxes in a furnace and I let out the molten metal into a damp mould. The result was an explosion of liquid aluminium in my face; my eyelids were stuck together with molten aluminium, solidified by the cold water thrown on me by my older brother. I believed I was blind and it hurt! The second time I was lucky that my brain has blocked out the experience by making me forget when I almost lost my life through a severe hypo! The third was on the M18 motorway where I still cannot comprehend what I experienced!

As I write these words, we are well into the year 2014. I still have the motorcycle and sidecar, I still have the battered ventriloquist's dummy, but I never got to cross the Humber Bridge.

Epilogue

Although unable to complete the challenge, our efforts were not in vain. We did manage to raise £3000.00 for the charity Living With a Lion, which continues raising money and awareness for the debilitating disease Diabetes.

Meanwhile, I've been keeping busy in the fund raising scheme of things. Just before Christmas 2013 I converted the sidecar into a sleigh, by covering it with red felt and trimming it with tinsel and fairy lights. The bike became Rudolf after I gave the headlamp a red cover, creating the 'Nose so bright' and attached antlers to the handlebars. I put on a Santa suit and took our collection buckets to put smiles on the faces of many, in return for their kind donations, while standing outside in the freezing cold at the Crystal Peaks shopping centre in Sheffield for several days in December. I did dress Charlie in an Elf's outfit and took him with me as Santa's little helper but he scared the kids.

We have every intention of continuing our fundraising and would love, one day to cross the Himalayas on our motorcycle and sidecar combination, which may take more than a smile when it comes to convincing the wives, especially seeing as we couldn't even cross the Humber Bridge.

Until such times, we expect to be organising shorter trips and hope to include other classic vehicles. Information will be posted on our website. livingwithalion.com which has a handy 'donation' button for you to press.

Thank you for reading my book, I hope it brought you at least a fraction of the enjoyment I experienced writing it.

Santa and his Sidecar Sleigh